Palgrave Studies in Political Marketing and Management

Series Editor
Jennifer Lees-Marshment
University of Auckland
Auckland, New Zealand

Palgrave Studies in Political Marketing and Management (PalPMM) series publishes high quality and ground-breaking academic research on this growing area of government and political behaviour that attracts increasing attention from scholarship, teachers, the media and the public. It covers political marketing intelligence including polling, focus groups, role play, co-creation, segmentation, voter profiling, stakeholder insight; the political consumer; political management including crisis management, change management, issues management, reputation management, delivery management; political advising; political strategy such as positioning, targeting, market-orientation, political branding; political leadership in all its many different forms and arena; political organization including managing a political office, political HR, internal party marketing; political communication management such as public relations and e-marketing and ethics of political marketing and management. For more information email the series editor Jennifer Lees-Marshment on j.lees-marshment@auckland. ac.nz and see https://leesmarshment.wordpress.com/pmm-book-series/.

More information about this series at
http://www.palgrave.com/gp/series/14601

Andrew Hughes

Market Driven Political Advertising

Social, Digital and Mobile Marketing

Andrew Hughes
Research School of Management
Australian National University
Canberra, ACT, Australia

Palgrave Studies in Political Marketing and Management
ISBN 978-3-319-77729-0   ISBN 978-3-319-77730-6   (eBook)
https://doi.org/10.1007/978-3-319-77730-6

Library of Congress Control Number: 2018936532

Cover pattern © Melisa Hasan

Printed on acid-free paper

This Palgrave Pivot imprint is published by the registered company Springer International
Publishing AG part of Springer Nature.
The registered company address is: Gewerbestrasse 11, 6330 Cham, Switzerland

For Danielle, Timothy and Benjamin, for everything, even the Lego on the floor

Acknowledgements

Firstly I would like to thank Prof. Jennifer Lees-Marshment for her support through this project and my career to date. Whilst many talk about leading the way, actions always express priorities and Jennifer has been brilliant in doing whatever she can to progress in the field of political marketing. Thank you, Jennifer.

Next to the publishers of this book, Palgrave Macmillan, thank you for supporting the field of political marketing. Without your willingness to support these types of projects many academics work would be hidden from view and society would be a poorer place without this knowledge being made available to all.

Thanks to all those who in some way shape or form who have helped me with ideas, advice and feedback for my research in this area. Prof. Phil Harris at Chester, you sir are a legend, Dr Stephen Dann for the early days, Prof. Aron O'Cass for showing that we Australians do indeed punch above our weight, and friends such as Dr Milos Gregor and Dr Ken Cosgrove for the global perspectives. To my colleagues at the Australian National University (ANU), including in political science, thank you for your encouragement for getting this done.

Thanks to those practitioners, some of who really would like to remain nameless, for your advice and suggestions for this book. It is you who get to implement what we write about and I hope that you find this book relevant and enjoyable.

To my extended family, thanks to Ross and Kathy for proofreading the early drafts of this—sorry again—and to my mum and dad for listening.

To Timothy and Benjamin, thank you my boys for letting Daddy finish this without suffering too many nerf gun injuries or Xbox fatalities. Finally, to my beautiful wife Danielle, thanks for everything that you did to make this easier for me and always being there—without you there could be no me.

Contents

LIST OF FIGURES

LIST OF TABLES

CHAPTER 1

Introduction and Outline

Abstract Chapter 1 outlines the overall idea and context of the book. This is how the current shift in methods used in political advertising from old or heritage media, such as television, radio and newspapers, to new or modern forms of media, such as websites, apps, mobile devices and platforms, and user-generated content is impacting on political communications and advertising.

It also provides a brief description on some key terms and contexts used, such as stakeholder marketing. There is also a brief overview of each chapter and how they fit into the overall approach of the book.

Keywords Introduction • Political marketing • Political advertising • Politics • Stakeholder

Political advertising as we know it from the past is dying. The new era of political advertising is about using digital and social media as a delivery mechanism of messages. The political advertising of campaigns past, delivered via older media methods such as television, print and radio, has lost much of its effectiveness as a tool even though there is still blind belief in it from some practitioners.

Instead political advertising has seen a rebirth in the mediums of the new millennium: social, digital and mobile. What we are seeing now is the very start of a new era in political advertising and its parent discipline of

© The Author(s) 2018   1
A. Hughes, *Market Driven Political Advertising*,
Palgrave Studies in Political Marketing and Management,
https://doi.org/10.1007/978-3-319-77730-6_1

political marketing. The new methods of political marketing are vehicles that are more effectively, more accurately and more interactively delivering political advertising messages at a micro-target or even individual level, something the old methods long dreamed of but could never accomplish.

They allow for a more effective integration of grassroots style campaigning as by its nature social media matches up perfectly to engaging a mass market in a more personalised and market driven way. These new methods of political advertising are no longer just delivering messages where we dwell, but wherever we happen to have access to media. They recognise we have moved from being involuntary receivers of message to being at times active information seekers and creators, voluntarily participating in the political communication process through how we may have created a news feed on one of our social media apps.

But digital and social media have also allowed for not just the rapid creation and delivery of political advertising, but the rapid creation and development of political brands, some of which either started on the internet, such as Italy's M5S, or heavily utilise digital methods and technology to act as disruptors in the market, such as the Pirate Party in nations such as Iceland and the Czech Republic.

The new political advertising methods and strategies, when used well, has made these brands come to life, offering more personalised and deeper engagement and experiences than what a one-directional advertisement on television could ever offer.

Yet there is a sense that political campaigning is still in need of reform and innovation. Whilst new media offers excitement and enthusiasm, this is more to do with the innovation of those specific platforms than anything that is happening in political advertising.

There still is an overuse of negative advertising and negative communications as a way of offering value to the consumer, yet the modern markets want more aspirational value offerings, they want to be engaged with in a positive way that gives them hope that their government and nations will be better places to live in. Negative advertising does not achieve that.

Political advertising on social media though is finally making the discipline take notice of a fact that it has long ignored: the role of information on advertising effectiveness. Far too many political advertisements in the past in old media campaigns were cram sessions of information, dumping information on consumers in a way that further alienated them from the brand and offered little chance of achieving any behavioural objectives through engagement and experience. One of the features of this book is how it will be amongst the first to explore the role of information on the effectiveness of political advertising, especially in the context of digital and social media.

This book cannot hope to cover all there is to know about political advertising, new or old, and that is not its aim. It only seeks to provide an analysis and overview of how some of the newer methods of political marketing and advertising are being used and what this may mean for stakeholders and society in the years ahead.

There is advice for practitioners, even a complete chapter dedicated to what practitioners can learn and use from the developments in social, digital and mobile marketing being used in campaigns around the world. Again, this is not a DIY guide on how to run a campaign, merely suggestions on what could work if a campaign wanted to use some of the aspects of those methods as discussed in this book.

It is also the author's hope that the following pages will provide a thought-provoking discussion on the implications for practitioners and academics of political advertising expanding into new horizons provided by the digital age. The author welcomes feedback and ideas on the areas discussed in this book. Most importantly it is wished that those reading this book do not regret doing so and enjoy the time they spend on the following pages.

OUTLINE

The following provides a brief abstract and outline of each chapter in the book.

Chapter 1 introduces the reader to the overall outline of the book and the content to be covered. It will outline the motivation for the book and what value the reader can expect to receive by reading and using the book.

Each chapter will be discussed in brief and provides an overall road map for the reader. Where necessary these outlines may provide some brief definitions that will help lay the foundation stones in the reader's mind of the conceptual, empirical and practitioner areas that will be covered by the book.

Chapter 2 outlines the theory behind exchange, value co-creation and a stakeholder perspective on political marketing. This is important in understanding why what we see in practice works and what doesn't as it is these foundational theories that support the use and reasoning behind the marketing communications used in a campaign.

A stakeholder perspective is important in political marketing as this does help explain why, as Lang (1991) so correctly identified, political advertising is a unique subset of integrated marketing communications. It also helps explain why advertising is targeted and used at some stakeholders, such as individual voters, yet for others other communication tools or public affairs methods are preferred.

Chapter 3 is by far the most theoretical chapter in the book. It is necessary though as it outlines some of the key theories in advertising, communications and political marketing. Understanding some of the theory behind advertising and communications will help you know why campaigns are starting to adopt social, digital and mobile political marketing.

It also explains and gives some examples of the different types of political advertising, like negative and positive advertising, and the importance of political advertising as a method of integrated political marketing communications.

It will discuss why, using the latest research that used psychophysiological methods, television advertising can no longer be used as the primary means of communication with an audience. There will be an examination and discussion of these findings for practitioners in the context of campaigns and the use of social, digital and mobile marketing.

Chapter 4 will examine how political advertising is being used on websites and social media. Whilst social media is broad, for the purposes of this book it will be categorised into those applications that use or incorporate video or dynamic advertisements and those that don't.

There will be a brief discussion on the emergence and growth in videography and image-sharing websites, such as YouTube and Facebook, and their importance as a communications tool.

After this there will be analysis and discussion of the three distinct subcategories that are emerging as areas of interest for those interested in political advertising and communications: video applications such as Vimeo, Facebook and YouTube; livecasting through Periscope and Facebook; and the multi-platform ways like Facebook, Twitter, Instagram and Snapchat.

This will be linked to the following section that will take a practitioner-focused approach by looking into the relationship between using these types of apps and developing higher levels of engagement, experience and interest in relationships with key stakeholders. It will be proposed that using this type of communication on these types of apps is allowing deeper and stronger relationships between consumers and political brands. Findings from evidence-based research and examples will be used to discuss the practical implications for practitioners and researchers.

Chapter 5 will look at how political advertising is moving from just one-directional mass communication traditional media to two-way communication and relationship building with new media. It also enables political organisations and candidates to obtain real-time data and feedback on policies and thus allows a much more market-driven approach.

This chapter will also examine how political advertising on social media is being used for awareness raising and to connect and engage with current and potential volunteers who may not be party members, something the Obama campaign pioneered in 2008.

There will be a discussion on how social media applications, when connected with a database programme, such as NationBuilder, allow for the rapid and direct use of volunteers, intelligence and information in a campaign. This integration of data from sources across multi-platforms, devices and applications is allowing for deeper insights into voting and consumer behaviour in the political marketplace, a trend which is assisting minor parties to compete with the larger brands. The chapter will conclude with a word of caution on the use of social media in these campaigns as seen through recent examples and experiences.

Chapter 6 will focus on the final aspect of the title of the book: mobile marketing. Mobile marketing is by far the highest spend in digital expenditure for many campaigns and uses a combination of older methods integrated with social and digital ones to achieve electoral outcomes for candidates and parties.

Next, the chapter discusses some of the methods campaigns have used over the last 20 years, with an emphasis on the Obama 2008 campaign as it was after this campaign that widespread adoption of the smart devices that many of us own today really took off.

Chapter 7 will act as a practitioner's overview of the content discussed so far, providing a brief description on how a political campaign could be run in the modern era based on some of the content and examples discussed in the book.

It is not intended to be a DIY guide on campaigning but rather to bring together some of the key concepts and lessons from previous chapters to provide advice and ideas for those who wish to run or analyse political campaigns from around the world.

It will conclude with some lessons from practice and how they can be implemented into a campaign.

Chapter 8 will be a very brief chapter and wrap up the ideas, thoughts and conclusions of the previous chapters to provide future research ideas for academics. Practitioners will also be provided with some ideas for future directions on how political advertising will continue to evolve in the dynamic consumer markets of 2018 and beyond as innovation in this area is mainly due to practitioners who think critically about how their campaigns could be better in the years ahead.

It will propose some new conceptual models for political advertising, branding and relationships that may provide some directions in the area for researchers and practitioners alike and start to get people thinking—"Do what we know now explains what happens now?"

Although political advertising was starting to lose its effectiveness in traditional media, especially with the proliferation of negative advertising, the way it has been adopted and used in new and social media indicates that its future is far from being dim: it is only getting brighter and brighter.

Finally, some notes on terminology. This book uses the term voter, voter consumer and consumer interchangeably but they all mean the same thing: the individual who turns up on election day and casts their vote. You can have your own opinion on what is the best one to use, but please keep this paragraph in mind as you go through the book and see these terms pop up.

As this book uses an actor-based stakeholder approach, occasionally other actors or stakeholders will be referred to as well. This means that an actor is a person or entity involved in an exchange with another actor. This could mean, for example, a voter exchanging value, their vote, with a political party in return for it implementing what it offered if elected. It could mean voters exchanging value with each other, or an industry group making a deal with the existing government for them to enact favourable legislation in exchange for their support at an election.

Each and every one reading this right now is an actor in an exchange, be they passive or active.

Therefore, stakeholders can be those actors who are not active in this exchange but may be impacted by it. For example, if a governing party offers to voters to reduce power bills if re-elected then the power companies that will be impacted by this change are the stakeholders who will be impacted by this decision. Chapter 2 will explain this in more detail.

So, with all of that out of the way, it is time. Now, let's do this.

Reference

Lang, A. (1991). Emotion, formal features, and memory for televised political advertisements. *Television and Political Advertising, 1,* 221–243.

CHAPTER 2

The Relationship Between Value Co-Creation, Exchange and Stakeholders

Abstract The relationship between stakeholders and political advertising has always been an important one but in the digital age that relationship is under threat from stakeholders with Machiavellian motives. This chapter outlines an actor-to-actor stakeholder-based conceptual model of value exchange in political marketing, which can be used to explain actor or stakeholder behaviour in any political system.

The chapter discusses the role of political marketing in a relationship marketing context. It looks into the influence which information from digital and social apps is having on strengthening existing relationships and developing new ones. The consequences on politics of this, such as the use of micro targeting strategies and database marketing through organisations such as Cambridge Analytica, is also examined.

Keywords Relationship marketing • CRM • Stakeholders • Political marketing • Exchange

Introduction

There is one reason why political advertising will always be required: to communicate value offerings to stakeholders.

Stakeholders, or actors, can be passive or active, and this classification will determine how a message is designed. The stakeholder themselves can vary

© The Author(s) 2018

A. Hughes, *Market Driven Political Advertising*,
Palgrave Studies in Political Marketing and Management,
https://doi.org/10.1007/978-3-319-77730-6_2

from an industry group to an individual. Essentially we are all stakeholders but each of us could be a multitude of different actors due to our lives and occupations. Just look at Superman—a mild-mannered reporter by day, a superhero by night.

However, what underpins the need for any advertising in the first place, be it to Superman or someone else, is the need to communicate an offering of an exchange. Sometimes this communication does not require any advertising at all, other forms of communications or public affairs (Harris and Sun 2017) can also perform this role.

For the purposes of this chapter though the focus will be on understanding how and what exchange is in a political marketing and advertising context, and how this exchange is created by stakeholders, but also influenced by others who may not be directly involved in it. So first things first—what is an exchange in a stakeholder context?

THE STAKEHOLDER MODEL OF VALUE OFFERINGS AND EXCHANGES IN POLITICAL MARKETING

Exchange and Political Marketing Communications

Explicit in the definition of marketing, and political marketing, is the communication of any offerings of value. Whilst communications can take many forms, television advertising is by far the most dominant method used in political campaigns due to its ability to reach several markets in a short space of time with messages of value exchanges. However, what television advertising is the most effective to use in a political marketing campaign has not been widely examined from the exchange perspectives of the promise of value or gain, and that of the promise of loss, or preventing something bad from happening or risk mitigation. Most research in this area has focused primarily on negative advertising's role in influencing voter turnout, attitude towards the brand and democracy (Marcus et al. 2000), and attack strategy, but not on what promise of exchange, be it loss (negative advertising) or value (positive advertising), is the most effective.

Prior research in political advertising has found contrasting findings when it comes to the use of negative advertising and liking towards the advertisement. Some studies, such as those by Merritt (1984) found negative advertising to be used as an information-gathering method by some voters and Pinkleton (1997) found that negative comparative advertising was effective at lowering the evaluations of attacked candidates whilst not harming the sponsoring brand. Lau and Rovner (2009) also identified a similar source credibility effect of negative advertising but from a practitioner perspective. They theorised that practitioners would risk using negative advertising even with a backlash effect if it meant that the net effect would be to harm their opponent and help their campaign. Fowler and Ridout (2013) more recently point to the fact that negative advertising is successful at getting media attention to a campaign and, therefore, free and credible publicity, highlighting another perspective on how the effectiveness of advertising can be measured.

However, there is also evidence that negative campaigning whilst memorable (Lau and Rovner 2009) is also perceived by voters negatively (Garramone 1984; Surlin and Gordon 1977) and may lower attitudes towards the sponsoring brand for its use (Garramone 1984; Garramone and Smith 1984). Other research (Lau and Rovner 2009; Lau et al. 2007) notes the lack of scientific research into negative advertising and support for its use. Lau et al.'s (2007) meta-analytic study of negative advertising found little scientific evidence for the use of negative advertising across several decades and methodologies. Yet it is still used and continues to be the preferred method of communications in election campaigns. As Lau and Rovner (2009) theorise perhaps this is because whilst several messages may not be effective, it only takes one message to work to achieve communication objectives and perhaps they could also be used more in a strategic sense, such as getting a response from the attacked party or influencing turnout, than in a communication sense.

From a promise of exchange and the definitional context, the use of negative advertising to communicate value is not supported (Hughes 2014, 2016). The very definition of marketing itself focuses on the creation of value and, even with the advent of Service Dominant Logic (SDL) and the actor-to-actor co-creation of value exchange (Lusch and Vargo 2012), value lies at the heart of exchange in marketing. The uniqueness of political marketing is located in the fact that dual exchanges are communicated—the exchange of loss that could occur, and the exchange of value being created with the market and stakeholders.

The promise of loss could be just as significant in influencing behaviour change as the promise of value, as this loss is linked to fear of experiencing long-term post-purchase cognitive dissonance. It is this exchange that could be the very reason why negative advertising is effective with some voters. In a close election where the result can be decided by narrow margins of a few percentage points, these voters could make all the difference between winning and losing. Although recall does not equate to liking, it does demonstrate top-of-mind awareness, which in turn makes the message more memorable, and easier to act upon, than other messages encountered. However, the efficacy of promise of positive gain versus the promise of a risk of loss through negative messaging is still unclear.

OFFERINGS OF VALUE

The offering of value is a critical classification in political marketing as value underlies all exchange models. Whilst the type and nature of an exchange can determine the value of a product, it is the communication of this value offering that is of most interest to political advertising researchers.

Offerings of value exist in political marketing as promises of value between the political party and the target market. For example, the offering from the political party may consist of future promises and the projected belief in the ability to govern based on the policy, leadership, candidate, party and prior track record (Hughes and Dann 2006a). Similarly, Harrop (1990), Grönroos (1990), Newman (1999a), Kotler and Kotler (1999), Lees-Marshment (2001a, b) and O'Shaughnessy (2001) support the notion of the political product as an intangible, abstract offering that has value for the voter and the broader society despite, as Egan (2005) points out, that exchange is often difficult to achieve when the party fails to win.

The political marketing literature recognises a range of offers of value between voter-actor and political party including the voter-actor offering votes, information, financial support and donations of time, effort and loyalty in return for the political actor offering value, such as effective governance, government by the voter-actor's preferred ideology, influence, support and preference (Scammell 1995; O'Cass 1996, 2001; Newman 1999a, b; Lees-Marshment 2001a, b; O'Shaughnessy 2001; Baines et al. 2002; Newman 2002; Hughes and Dann 2006a, b; Hughes 2007).

Other exchanges in political marketing that take place will be dependent upon the other actor in the exchange. Whilst Ormrod et al. (2013) see exchange as triadic in nature, this is contrary to Vargo and Lusch (2004a) and Lusch and Vargo (2012) who see no such restriction on how an exchange can take place insofar as any actor in the political market can exchange value with any other actor in the same political market.

Regardless of the type or nature of exchange, by far the exchange of most interest to researchers and practitioners is always going to be between the voter-actor and the political entity. As most voter-actors have low involvement and interest in politics, obtaining awareness of the value offering is the first step in any process of communicating with this segment.

Within the political marketing process, marketing communications also provide a social information framework to assist the consumer in their self-identification with the political brand (Robinson 2004; Reeves et al. 2006). As political marketing communications are faced with a similar competitive situation for consumer attention amidst competing counter messages and rebuttal messages, they must create value for the voter consumer (Jackson 2005).

Political marketers have identified information, tribal identity through branding and vicarious victory through negative campaigns discrediting perceived political opponents, as potential offers of value to be communicated to voters. Information-based advertising offers rationality, and the link between the consumer's self-perception as an "issues voter" and their pursuit of policy knowledge (Andreasen 1995, 2006; Kotler et al. 2002; Chen and Chen 2003; Sanders and Norris 2005).

Tribal identity and loyalty through the development of a strong brand, and the social messages from the brand association, can be potential exchanges of value (Bauer et al. 1996; Hughes 2003, 2004; Chen and Chen 2003; Egan 2005; Ingram and Lees-Marshment 2002; O'Shaughnessy and Henneberg 2007; Scammell 2007; Dann and Hughes 2008). For example, Barack Obama's 2008 US Presidential campaign was partly built around the campaign theme of Hope, and Kevin Rudd in 2007 built part of his value offering around the experience of voters being engaged and connected with the Kevin07 campaign (Dann and Hughes 2008).

Tribal reinforcement is an emotional response which is consistent with a self-identification as a "Values Voter", where the message's perceived adherence to a shared set of beliefs is valued by the consumer. The concept of tribal loyalty can be linked to brand communities (Eagar 2012) and relationships between brands and brand communities (Algesheimer et al. 2005), and also the broader marketing theories of brand preference, attitude and loyalty. Baker et al. (1986) found that the more familiar a consumer was with a brand, the more likely they were to purchase that brand, perceive it positively, motivate purchase behaviour and have it in their evoked set. The concept is touched on in a political sense by Gruszczynski et al.'s (2013) research into the relationship between arousing images and political participation. They found that those who were more physiologically aroused by a full range of negative and positive images were also more likely to be involved or engaged in politics.

Vicarious victory is the emotional satisfaction received when viewing negative campaign messages about disliked opponents. Negative messages play a reinforcing and supporting role for those opposing the person being discredited (Bissell 1994; Hughes 2003; Dean 2005; Sanders and Norris 2005; O'Shaughnessy and Henneberg 2007). Negative advertising is also designed to raise perceived social costs of support for a candidate thus raising the level of involvement and cognitive processing involvement in the decision. As an offer of value, it may also be used as a reinforcement to the values voter to confirm their "in-group" status versus the "out-group" status of the sponsor of the attacking message.

Other aspects of idea product distribution previously regarded as promotional mix elements can be seen to deliver "offerings that have value". For example, publication of propaganda, political statements and "talking points" that assist the individual voter in persuading others to support their position can be an offering of value to a political blogger seeking content to republish to their readership (McMillan and Morrison 2006) or the online activist seeking to debate others (Rosen 2006).

Communications strategies such as branded political websites (Hughes and Dann 2006a), policy announcement sites (Ireland and Nash 2001) and celebrity endorsements (Hughes and Dann 2006b) can create offerings of value for the consumer seeking reassurance that their political position is supported by other community members (Blanchfield 2006; Dann and Hughes 2008; Rinehart 2008).

The combination of exchange and "offerings that have value" incorporate the customer co-creation process, dialogue-based marketing, permission marketing and customer engagement in the marketing process into the product development and marketing communications phases. Co-creation of value through either services or embedded services has been a hallmark of the service dominant logic whereby the value is created through the customer's use of a product or service (Vargo and Lusch 2004a, b, 2008).

The American Marketing Association's (2013) definition builds on the co-creation platform by recognising inter-customer exchange as a means of creation, communication and delivery of value, which can be utilised by social marketing for developing community-driven solutions, social norms, cultural and symbolic meanings for brands, and the interpretation of social marketing messages into ideas, values and beliefs. From a political marketing perspective, co-creation has had limited development beyond Granik's (2005) customer co-creation of value in political marketing parties and Scammell's (2007) discussion of co-created political branding.

Another element of the American Marketing Association's (2013) definition of value to this thesis is the four target groups who are the recipients of the outcomes of the marketing process. Customers are the recipients of direct value from the political process in exchange for their time, effort, votes or cash which includes voters, active party supporters and current party members (Ormrod et al. 2007).

Clients are those people who are the indirect beneficiaries of a policy or government action even if they did not vote for the political party. As political products are produced for the open market, they are consumed by the client/customer target market (potential voters, actual voters) and the partner market (opposing political parties, opposing voters, media and related groups) (Hughes and Dann 2006b).

Partners then, in this context, are the active participants in the political marketing process. This covers the suppliers and distributors of the political marketing product and may include the media and other parties within the political playing field. Society at large represents the whole of the community as a stakeholder in the political process (Dean and Croft 2001; Ormrod et al. 2007). Whilst individual stakeholder clusters can be addressed through segmentation strategies, Egan (2005) and Baines et al. (2013) emphasise the difference between commercial and political marketing in that the end result of successful political marketing is the need to address the needs of all stakeholders whilst in office.

THE ROLE OF LOSS IN POLITICAL MARKETING EXCHANGE

The role of loss in exchange has only recently become of interest to marketers as they start to redetermine the definition and role of exchange into a concept that can be more readily applied to the practice of marketing and is less concerned with the economics of marketing (Sheth and Uslay 2007). Sheth and Uslay (2007) make the point that exchange paradigm is driven by self-interest, which results in a win-loss scenario whereby the organisation benefits at the consumer's expense.

They highlight the move away from value being created to meet a need to being more of co-creation, driven by both actors in the process. This actor-to-actor concept has been further developed and expanded on by Lusch and Vargo (2012) in their work. This actor-to-actor exchange model of Lusch and Vargo (2012) means that marketing is no longer concerned with the economics of exchange, but more the broader paradigm and context in which exchange can develop and evolve in the context of a unique transaction, encapsulating as Sheth and Uslay (2007) note all aspects of the marketing function.

In a political context what this means is that if marketing exchange can be seen from a co-creation perspective as Sheth and Uslay (2007), Vargo and Lusch (2004a) and Lusch and Vargo (2012) have stated and if the consumer is receiving a negative value in exchange from the organisation or other actor as a result of the co-creation process then this can make that exchange one of loss for the consumer. For example, if a voter votes for a party that then loses an election then the exchange has not been of value as that party is less likely to be able to implement the policies that it offered the voter as it is not in a position to govern.

Conversely, if a party allowed voters to co-create policies with it but then those policies were altered due to the role of other stakeholders in the exchange process then the exchange will have been one of loss for those consumers. An organisation actor may also experience loss from a voter if that voter decides to change their vote to another actor and thereby make it difficult for a political organisation to achieve long-term societal, political and economic reform that it may have thought possible when it co-created value with the voter initially.

The definition of political marketing exchange needs to reflect this notion of co-created value having the potential of containing loss and not just value. Therefore the definition of political marketing exchange is:

An exchange between two actors in political markets and networks that are active and dynamic in co-creating, service provisioning and resource integrating offerings of value with one another that will obtain each a net gain.

The concept of value co-creation in politics may be hard to conceptualise as it could be argued that political parties only offer value, they do not co-create it. But this would only be the case if the role of stakeholders in politics was ignored, which is impractical and not realistic of how modern politics functions in most political markets around the globe (Hughes and Dann 2009).

STAKEHOLDERS IN POLITICAL MARKETING

The relationship between stakeholders, public affairs and politics is well established (Hughes and Dann 2009). Stakeholder groups have increasingly turned to public affairs to achieve their objectives, and for some public affairs firms they may represent different stakeholders on the one issue or even act as a facilitator on an issue to achieve key objectives for all sides. As Getz (2001) noted there is a need for further research into the relationship between a stakeholder's objectives, firm objectives and public affairs.

While it could be argued that the rise of stakeholders could also be attributed to a weakening or lack of democratic political systems, this can be countered by the fact that actors in political markets in all parts of the world, if anything more in democracies, have benefitted from engaging and exchanging with other actors who value the speed and direct action that a value exchange in political marketing affords.

The Political Marketing Stakeholder Model

Stakeholders in political marketing can be classified using a modified five-attribute model based on the work of Mitchell et al. (1997). These five attributes are power, legitimacy, urgency, relationship and value. These attributes take into consideration the importance of relationships in business, political and social contexts and also the importance of the value that stakeholders seek to exchange in an actor-to-actor model which typifies that which is already seen in public affairs (Table 2.1).

These attributes can be used to build a conceptual framework on which to assess the influence of individual stakeholders in either a broad or specific context regardless of political system or voting methods.

Understanding the contextual nature of stakeholders in a political exchange allows a picture to be constructed of how a certain stakeholder, or group of stakeholders, may behave in one country as compared to another. This allows a comparison across political, business and social systems and to understand what value is being sought by stakeholders in different countries.

For example, a mining company may be active in certain countries at a certain time in south-east Asia as the value they derive may be higher, relationships stronger and more powerful. However, there could also be a greater sense of urgency due to changing power arrangements in government and society in one nation that could change the nature of the exchange and the relationship rapidly (Fig. 2.1).

Table 2.1   Stakeholder exchange-based attribute model definitions

Attribute	Definition	Based on
Power	"A relationship among social actors in which one social actor, A, can get another social actor, B, to do something that B would not"	Dahl (1957), Pfeffer (1981), Weber (1947), Hester et al. (2012)
Legitimacy	"A generalized perception or assumption that the actions of an entity are desirable, proper, or appropriate within some socially constructed system of norms, values, beliefs, definitions" (Mitchell et al. 1997: 869)	Weber (1947)
Urgency	"The degree to which stakeholder claims for immediate attention" (Mitchell et al. 1997: 869)	Mitchell et al. (1997)
Relationship	The level and intensity to which the actors have a connection, either past or present, and the length of time that such a connection has existed.	Grönroos (1984), Gummesson (1994)
Value	Value is co-created in the exchange between actors, always determined by the beneficiary, and may be experiential, contextual and meaning-laden.	Vargo and Lusch (2004a, 2008)

RELATIONSHIP MARKETING

A Brief Background

Once marketers realised that they didn't need to be confined by a set number of marketing elements, or letter of the alphabet, they realised that it was more important to think about the different paradigms, or ways, that marketing could be applied.

One of these ways had long been in existence and use in many parts of the world: relationship marketing. Famous trade routes, such as the Silk Road between China, India and Europe, were built on relationships and were critical in forging not just business ties but also diplomatic ones as relationships were maintained for hundreds of years.

Relationship marketing as a practice goes back literally thousands of years, but as a theory and studied area of marketing it is relatively modern. Some (Grönroos 1991) refer to this area of marketing as the "Scandinavian School of Marketing" because of the importance of relationship marketing in this region of the world, but it may also be possibly because one of its earliest and leading theorists, Christian Grönroos, comes from Finland.

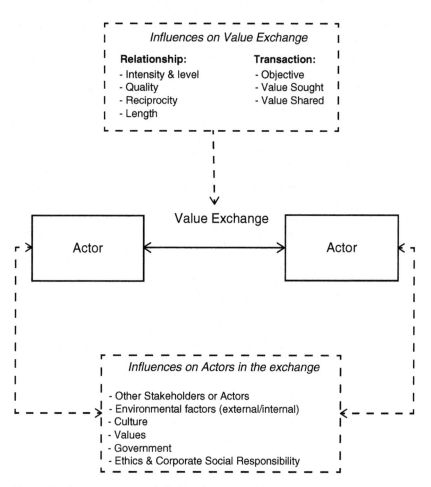

Fig. 2.1 Actor-to-actor stakeholder-based model of value exchange in political marketing (Hughes 2016)

So what is relationship marketing really? Relationship marketing places the emphasis on a long-term interactive relationship that is beneficial to both actors in the exchange which is supported by marketing activities (Grönroos 1994). Relationship marketing therefore is a way of thinking and approaching all marketing, including the individual activities and tactics. It places the relationship with the customer, and indeed other stakeholders, as being of primary importance.

Relationship marketing is concerned with two primary activities: attracting the customer and then building and enhancing that relationship over a long period of time (Grönroos 1994). The higher the level of trust in the relationship, the higher the amount of value both will place on that relationship. As a long-term perspective is taken, relationship marketing is less concerned with short-term transactions, even if they occur at a loss, as the lifetime value of the relationship is considered more important.

Relationship marketing therefore redefines value away from a purely economic or financial context to a more customer-centric view of value on the relationship itself, while still recognising the importance of profitability in all relationships through effective customer relationship management (CRM) methods.

Does relationship marketing therefore use a marketing mix? No, relationship marketing moves away from a mixed approach to a more functional or tactic-based approach where any marketing activity or method can be used so long as that can support the relationship between brand and consumer.

One of the most important activities marketers use in relationship marketing are loyalty programmes. Using a standard marketing approach would be classified as a promotional method. Loyalty programmes can be as simple as a card stamped and then rewarding a customer with a free product based on frequency of usage, for example, every fifth coffee free, or as complex as an airline or a bank's loyalty programme that is linked into a database.

For politics loyalty will depend on the stakeholder and the unique characteristics of their relationship with the actor offering value. For example, perhaps a lobbyist can obtain more concessions on behalf of their client because they once worked together, or perhaps a local party member who put signs in their yard during an election will get their road fixed sooner than others.

As technology advances rapidly, loyalty programmes are moving onto mobile and cloud databases, moving with the consumer and being linked to more and more information that drive closer and more in-depth insights about consumers than has ever existed in the history of mankind. This is one example of how these newer marketing paradigms that are emerging, such as relationship marketing, are using whatever marketing tactics and activities that are necessary to create, deliver and support the value exchange and relationship between consumer and brand.

Political Marketing and Relationship Marketing

By its very nature relationship marketing is already integrated into every aspect of political marketing. Relationship marketing does not follow a theoretical or practical rule book when it comes to what methods or strategies of marketing to use as the centre of all activities is the development, maintenance and strengthening of the relationship between actors.

If anything the dominant marketing paradigm in politics is relationship marketing. Safe seats are so because of a strong relationship between community and brand built and reinforced through generations of mutual exchanges of value, marginal seats show that there are a small proportion of people who have no relationship or identification with any party that is strong enough to lead to a sustainable loyalty. In some political systems relationship marketing has replaced democracy or was preferred over it because this allowed for a more compatible system of government with that nation's culture. This is not to say that relationships can also lead to the concentration of power in the hands of very few or the development of flawed policy or other negative behaviours, but these issues with relationship marketing can and do happen anywhere.

Relationship marketing long ago threw out the rule book on the use of a marketing mix or following a certain paradigm of certain thinking. The relationship is clearly front and centre and marketing methods are used as appropriate to that relationship. However, creating and developing that relationship in politics in the modern era means that political brands need to adapt and change to offer value across multi-constructs and offerings. Simply hoping that pork barrelling is going to be enough to create a long-lasting relationship is not going to lead to a sustainable relationship, as the stakeholder model discussed above demonstrates.

These value constructs in a political relationship will include engagement, experience and emotional response, leading to a resonance and relationship with the brand that goes beyond skin deep. Change campaigns and movements try and tap into these constructs as the key part of their value offering, rarely are financial motives used to change behaviour or to develop relationships in these cases. It is all about value being based around the intangible aspects of the relationship.

Whilst some modern work on stakeholders in political marketing has considered the issue of theoretical constructs they do not consider what evidence does: that by its very nature a relationship is fluid and usually built around more intangible, pragmatic and realistic offerings of value. If the word customer is substituted for actor, a more appropriate term according to Vargo and Lusch (2004a), relationships in politics can be understood in a more evidenced-supported context. Ormrod and Henneberg (2010) note that a looking-beyond-the-customer approach is needed in politics, but it has always existed as the relationship has always ruled in political marketing.

Lees-Marshment's (2014) idea of partners in politics has far more relevance to what is actually happening in politics and in marketing at large as this supports the notion of the wider concept of co-creation of value in an exchange between two willing actors that has underlied relationship marketing for aeons. It also helps in explaining the proactive nature of voter consumers in creating content that support a brand: no party out there sends out a daily request for supporters to create gifs and memes on social media, they do that because they want to, as a form of offering in the relationship they have with multiple stakeholders.

This idea of multiple stakeholder exchanges is not just unique to politics but is a feature of it and can help explain why still to this day television advertising is the most preferred method of communicating offerings of value. That is, it can connect with a whole range of markets and actors that a political brand may be in relationship with in an effective way. Social media allows for the communication of value offerings in those more individual relationships where the advertisement can be tailored just for that particular exchange.

Relationship marketing in politics does need far more research and investigation as this will help provide future directions on how political advertising may evolve further in the future based in both heritage and new media platforms.

Heritage and New Media: Some Perspectives on Political Advertising

With social media now being so widely used around the world, political advertising has new distribution channels to reach further and deeper into markets in political marketing campaigns. In the era of the permanent campaign (Needham 2005) social media has also become the dominant method for advertising and communications, perhaps none better demonstrated by the use of Twitter by US President Donald Trump.

The era of social media has allowed political advertising to move from being just about raising awareness of value offerings during campaign periods to acting as an enabler of relationship creation, stakeholder management and engagement, and of course creating excitement and viral buzz through policy or leader announcements.

Through social media political advertising has kept its ability to influence emotions with the new generations, such as Gen Y and the millennials, and the information-intense era that has altered how we all consume media.

Another significant influence of social media on the use and impact of political advertising in political campaigns has been on resources and people. Previously, traditional media acted as a barrier for minor parties seeking to challenge the status quo, with high production costs and access to mainstream media being out of the reach of many a minor party.

Social media changed all of that. It gave more power and influence back to minor parties, especially those that were prepared to have a more market-based focus, and the lower costs and live broadcasting on apps such as Facebook or YouTube allowed these parties to rival some of the campaigns being run by larger and more organised parties.

That is not to say, however, that political advertising in the more traditional or heritage formats of television, radio, print and outdoor is less effective at increasing awareness, just that it is ineffective at meeting those objectives for an increasing number of segments that now rely upon other media and communication to obtain information about politics. This has been highlighted in the 2016 US Presidential and other election races that highlighted how susceptible some consumers were to fake news websites, and also in the Australian 2016 Federal election where a fake scare campaign was instrumental in swaying some late undecided voters to swing their vote to the Labor opposition.

These trends also point to another important trend in modern political advertising: the importance of information in elections. Annie Lang's (2000) widely accepted model of limited capacity for message processing found that every person has only a limited capacity at any one time in which to process a message. This capacity can vary due to a number of factors, such as age, occupation, amount of sleep, memory utilised, the task being performed, the relevance of information and the complexity of the information to be processed.

An acknowledgement of the impact of the information age is how much of a person's recall is now outsourced through search engines such as Google ("Just Google It" is acknowledged as a formal phrase) and YouTube or stored electronically in the cloud through file and data storage pro-grammes, or even how management of social lives has been delegated to social media.

This impact is only slowly being noticed by political advertising practitioners. If anything social media ads should be the base for political ads in the future in terms of how much information should be contained in a 30-second television spot. With trends on early voting behaviour demonstrating that more and more people in democracies are casting their votes as early as possible, political advertising needs to start to adapt and change to this fundamental shift in how actors have already consumed political information to the point that they can make their decisions far earlier in a campaign.

If anything this should mean a change of strategy from the last 7–10 days 30% spend of total budget to moving that to the front of the campaign and then allowing for more issue-specific advertisements as the campaign evolves. Then in the final week there should be more reminders of value offerings than pleading-style advertisements, but with all that said there is need for more research into voting behaviour that occurs before polling days. One thing is for sure that the information age is here and political advertising needs to hurry up and get a move on to keep up with how information is being created, designed and consumed in this era.

References

Algesheimer, R., Dholakia, U. M., & Herrmann, A. (2005). The social influence of brand community: Evidence from European car clubs. *Journal of Marketing, 69*(3), 19–34.

American Marketing Association. (2013). Definition of marketing. Retrieved July 15, 2013, from http://www.marketingpower.com/AboutAMA/Pages/DefinitionofMarketing.aspx

Andreasen, A. R. (1995). *Marketing social change*. San Francisco, CA: Jossey-Bass.

Andreasen, A. R. (2006). *Social marketing in the 21st century*. Thousand Oaks, CA: Sage.

Baines, P., Crawford, I., O'Shaughnessy, N., Worcester, R., & Mortimore, R. (2013). Positioning in political marketing: How semiotic analysis adds value to traditional survey approaches. *Journal of Marketing Management, 30*(1–2), 172–200.

Baines, P. R., Harris, P., & Lewis, B. R. (2002). The political marketing planning process: Improving image and message in strategic target areas. *Marketing Intelligence and Planning, 20*(1), 6–14.

Baker, W., Hutchinson, J. W., Moore, D., & Nedungadi, P. (1986). Brand familiarity and advertising: Effects on the evoked set and brand preference. *Advances in Consumer Research, 13*(1), 637–642.

Bauer, H. H., Huber, F., & Herrmann, A. (1996). Political marketing: An information-economic analysis. *European Journal of Marketing, 30*(10/11), 152–165.

Bissell, J. (1994, November 21). Politics may be negative, but not brand marketing. *Brandweek*, p. 16.

Blanchfield, T. A. (2006). Culture and politics. *Campaigns and Elections, 27*(6), 59.

Chen, C.-F., & Chen, J.-M. (2003). The construction of electoral marketing modes in Taiwan. *International Journal of Management, 20*(2), 143–155.

Dahl, R. A. (1957). The concept of power. *Systems Research and Behavioral Science, 2*(3), 201–215.

Dann, S., & Hughes, A. (2008). Australian political marketing after Kevin07: Lessons from the 2007 federal election. *Monash Business Review, 4*(1), 34–37.

Dean, D., & Croft, R. (2001). Friends and relations: Long-term approaches to political campaigning. *European Journal of Marketing, 35*(11/12), 1197–1217.

Dean, J. (2005). Communicative capitalism: Circulation and the foreclosure of politics. *Cultural Politics, 1*(1), 51–74.

Eagar, T. (2012), *Moderating influences in intracommunity brand engagement: Brand faces and brand heroes performance on the brand stage*. PhD thesis, Australian National University.

Egan, J. (2005). Another false dawn? The liberal democrats 2005. *Journal of Marketing Management, 21*(9–10), 959–978.

Fowler, E. F., & Ridout, T. N. (2013). Negative, angry, and ubiquitous: Political advertising in 2012. *The Forum, 10*(4), 51–61.

Garramone, G. M. (1984). Voter responses to negative political ads. *Journalism and Mass Communication Quarterly, 61*(2), 250–259.

Garramone, G. M., & Smith, S. J. (1984). Reactions to political advertising: Clarifying sponsor effects. *Journalism and Mass Communication Quarterly, 61*(4), 771–775.

Getz, K. A. (2001). Public affairs and political strategy: Theoretical foundations. *Journal of Public Affairs, 1*(4), 305–329.

Granik, S. (2005). A reconceptualisation of the antecedents of party activism: A multidisciplinary approach. *Political Studies, 53*(3), 598–620.

Grönroos, C. (1984). A service quality model and its marketing implications. *European Journal of Marketing, 18*(4), 36–44.

Grönroos, C. (1990). Relationship approach to marketing in service contexts: The marketing and organizational behavior interface. *Journal of Business Research*, 20(1), 3–11.

Grönroos, C. (1991). The marketing strategy continuum: Towards a marketing concept for the 1990s. *Management Decision*, 29(1), 7–13.

Grönroos, C. (1994). Quo Vadis, marketing? Toward a relationship marketing paradigm. *Journal of Marketing Management*, 10(5), 347–360.

Gruszczynski, M. W., Balzer, A., Jacobs, C. M., Smith, K. B., & Hibbing, J. R. (2013). The physiology of political participation. *Political Behavior*, 35(1), 135–152.

Gummesson, E. (1994). Making relationship marketing operational. *International Journal of Service Industry Management*, 5(5), 5–20.

Harris, P., & Sun, H. (2017). The ends justify the means: A global research agenda for political marketing and public affairs. *Journal of Public Affairs*, 17(4).

Harrop, M. (1990). Political marketing. *Parliamentary Affairs*, 43(3), 277–291.

Hester, K. S., Robledo, I. C., Barrett, J. D., Peterson, D. R., Hougen, D. P., Day, E. A., & Mumford, M. D. (2012). Causal analysis to enhance creative problem-solving: Performance and effects on mental models. *Creativity Research Journal*, 24(2–3), 115–133.

Hughes, A. (2003). Can branding theory be applied to marketing political parties? A case study of the Australian Greens. In *Australian and New Zealand Marketing Academy*, Adelaide, Australia, 1–3 December.

Hughes, A. (2004). The power and the passion: Will celebrity candidates become the norm in future political marketing campaigns. In *International Nonprofit and Social Marketing Conference*.

Hughes, A. (2007). Personal brands: An exploratory analysis of personal brands in Australian political marketing. In *Australia and New Zealand Marketing Academy Conference*, 3–5 December, University of Otago, Dunedin, New Zealand.

Hughes, A. (2016). Why negative political ads don't work on Gen Y. In *Advances in Consumer Research* (Vol. 44).

Hughes, A., & Dann, S. (2006a). Political marketing 2006: Direct benefit, value and managing the voter relationship. In *Australia and New Zealand Marketing Academy Conference*, 4–6 December, Brisbane, QLD, Australia.

Hughes, A., & Dann, S. (2006b). Political marketing and stakeholders. In *Australia and New Zealand Marketing Academy Conference*, 4–6 December, Brisbane, QLD, Australia.

Hughes, A., & Dann, S. (2009). Political marketing and stakeholder engagement. *Marketing Theory*, 9(2), 243–256.

Ingram, P., & Lees-Marshment, J. (2002). The anglicisation of political marketing: How Blair 'out-marketed' Clinton. *Journal of Public Affairs*, 2(2), 44–56.

Ireland, E., & Nash, P. T. (2001). *Winning campaigns online: Strategies for candidates and causes.* Bethesda, MD: Science Writers Press.

Jackson, N. (2005). Vote winner or a nuisance: Email and elected politicians' relationship with their constituents. *Journal of Nonprofit & Public Sector Marketing, 14*(1–2), 91–108.

Kotler, P., & Kotler, N. (1999). Political marketing: Generating effective candidates, campaigns, and causes. In *Handbook of political marketing* (pp. 3–18). Thousand Oaks, CA: Sage.

Kotler, P., Roberto, N., & Lee, N. R. (2002). *Social marketing: Improving the quality of life.* Thousand Oaks, CA: Sage.

Lang, A. (2000). The limited capacity model of mediated message processing. *Journal of Communication, 50*(1), 46–70.

Lau, R. R., & Rovner, I. B. (2009). Negative campaigning. *Annual Review of Political Science, 12*, 285–306.

Lau, R. R., Sigelman, L., & Rovner, I. B. (2007). The effects of negative political campaigns: A meta-analytic reassessment. *Journal of Politics, 69*(4), 1176–1209.

Lees-Marshment, J. (2001a). The marriage of politics and marketing. *Political Studies, 49*(4), 692–713.

Lees-Marshment, J. (2001b). The product, sales and market-oriented party-how labour learnt to market the product, not just the presentation. *European Journal of Marketing, 35*(9/10), 1074–1084.

Lees-Marshment, J. (2014). *Political marketing: Principles and applications.* Routledge.

Lusch, R. F., & Vargo, S. L. (2012). The forum on markets and marketing (FMM) advancing service-dominant logic. *Marketing Theory, 12*(2), 193–199.

Marcus, G. E., Russell Neuman, W., & MacKuen, M. (2000). *Affective intelligence and political judgment.* Chicago: University of Chicago Press.

Merritt, S. (1984). Negative political advertising: Some empirical findings. *Journal of Advertising, 13*(3), 27–38.

McMillan, S. J., & Morrison, M. (2006). Coming of age with the internet: A qualitative exploration of how the internet has become an integral part of young people's lives. *New Media & Society, 8*(1), 73–95.

Mitchell, R. K., Agle, B. R., & Wood, D. J. (1997). Toward a theory of stakeholder identification and salience: Defining the principle of who and what really counts. *Academy of Management Review, 22*(4), 853–886.

Needham, C. (2005). Brand leaders: Clinton, Blair and the limitations of the permanent campaign. *Political Studies, 53*(2), 343–361.

Newman, B. I. (1999a). *Handbook of political marketing.* Thousand Oaks, CA: Sage.

Newman, B. I. (1999b). *The mass marketing of politics: Democracy in an age of manufactured images.* Thousand Oaks, CA: Sage.

Newman, B. (2002). The role of marketing in politics. *Journal of Political Marketing, 1*(1), 1–5.

O'Cass, A. (1996). Political marketing and the marketing concept. *European Journal of Marketing, 30*(10/11), 37–53.

O'Cass, A. (2001). Political marketing-an investigation of the political marketing concept and political market orientation in Australian politics. *European Journal of Marketing, 35*(9/10), 1003–1025.

Ormrod, R. P., & Henneberg, S. C. (2010). An investigation into the relationship between political activity levels and political market orientation. *European Journal of Marketing, 44*(3/4), 382–400.

Ormrod, R. P., Henneberg, S. C., Forward, N., Miller, J., & Tymms, L. (2007). Political marketing in untraditional campaigns: The case of David Cameron's Conservative Party leadership victory. *Journal of Public Affairs, 7*(3), 235–248.

Ormrod, R. P., Henneberg, S. C. M., & O'Shaughnessy, N. J. (2013). *Political marketing: Theory and concepts.* Sage Publications Limited.

O'Shaughnessy, N. (2001). The marketing of political marketing. *European Journal of Marketing, 35*(9/10), 1047–1057.

O'Shaughnessy, N., & Henneberg, S. (2007). The selling of the President 2004: A marketing perspective. *Journal of Public Affairs, 7*(3), 249–268.

Pfeffer, J. (1981). *Power in organizations* (Vol. 33). Marshfield, MA: Pitman.

Pinkleton, B. (1997). The effects of negative comparative political advertising on candidate evaluations and advertising evaluations: An exploration. *Journal of Advertising, 26*(1), 19–29.

Reeves, P., de Chernatony, L., & Carrigan, M. (2006). Building a political brand: Ideology or voter-driven strategy. *The Journal of Brand Management, 13*(6), 418–428.

Rinehart, D. (2008). Baby talk: How gender issues affected media coverage of the child-care debate in the last federal election. *Canadian Journal of Media Studies, 4*(1), 1–40.

Robinson, J. (2004). Repackaging our politicians. *NZ Marketing Magazine, 23*(5), 12–19.

Rosen, J. (2006, June 27). The people formerly known as the audience. *Pressthink.*

Sanders, D., & Norris, P. (2005). The impact of political advertising in the 2001 UK general election. *Political Research Quarterly, 58*(4), 525–536.

Scammell, M. (1995). *Designer politics: How elections are won.* London: Macmillan.

Scammell, M. (2007). Political brands and consumer citizens: The rebranding of Tony Blair. *The Annals of the American Academy of Political and Social Science, 611*(1), 176–192.

Sheth, J. N., & Uslay, C. (2007). Implications of the revised definition of marketing: From exchange to value creation. *Journal of Public Policy & Marketing, 26*(2), 302–307.

Surlin, S. H., & Gordon, T. F. (1977). How values affect attitudes toward direct reference political advertising. *Journalism and Mass Communication Quarterly, 54*(1), 89–98.

Vargo, S. L., & Lusch, R. F. (2004a). Evolving to a new dominant logic for marketing. *Journal of Marketing, 68*(1), 1–17.

Vargo, S. L., & Lusch, R. F. (2004b). The four service marketing myths remnants of a goods-based, manufacturing model. *Journal of Service Research, 6*(4), 324–335.

Vargo, S. L., & Lusch, R. F. (2008). Why 'service'? *Journal of the Academy of Marketing Science, 36*(1), 25–38.

Weber, M. (1947). *The theory of economic and social organization* (A. M. Henderson & T. Parsons, Trans.). New York: Oxford University Press.

CHAPTER 3

The Theory and the Practice of Political Advertising

Abstract After reading the foundational importance of the exchange process and stakeholders to political advertising, it is now time to strap yourselves in as this chapter contains the theory on the why, how, what, when and where of advertising effectiveness in a political marketing context.

Whilst containing a lot of background theory about advertising and political advertising, it does provide the necessary knowledge important in understanding how advertising can be effective. It enables the reader to be able to critically assess and ask how the modern methods so widely used are achieving their objectives, and how they could also be used against stakeholders by those with ulterior motives.

Keywords Political advertising • Digital marketing • Social media • Mobile marketing • Political marketing

Introduction

Political advertising is being reborn. There is no sole reason for this. Many reasons have helped revitalise and change the perception of political advertising from being a blunt tool of the past to the weapon of the new micro-segmented campaign.

© The Author(s) 2018
A. Hughes, *Market Driven Political Advertising*,
Palgrave Studies in Political Marketing and Management,
https://doi.org/10.1007/978-3-319-77730-6_3

One of the biggest reasons has been the continuous rise of social media. Social media's power as a communication tool in multiple contexts and constructs is well documented, be it from communication, campaigning, behaviour change to being a source of information.

Although the use of social media is nothing new in political campaigns, what has changed in recent times and has turned it into a formidable method of persuasion is the integration and use of big data to allow for highly personalised targeting and engagement of micro-segments which once would have been impossible.

This targeting strategy has moved some segments from awareness to devoted loyalists in such a short span of time which even the most optimistic (or pessimistic) political science data modelling failed to predict. This is because the advertising was closely tied to the issues that mattered the most to that segment, connecting value offering to behaviour that more traditional methods could not offer. This chapter will explore how the use of big data has changed the use, methods and strategies for political advertising.

Next, this chapter will consider the relationship between political brands and political advertising. The use of digital political advertising methods has allowed for political brands to create deeper and higher levels of emotional responses through personalised messaging.

Along with incorporating more and more mainstream methods of marketing, such as low-risk "populist" policies that offer simplistic ways of understanding the policy, candidates chosen to resemble the target market, and experiential opportunities such as events in the round, political brands are more aware than ever of the need to maintain a strong brand resonance with key markets through developing unique brand personalities. These brand personalities in themselves may vary with each market but they will be consistent with the brand platform as a whole.

IS POLITICAL ADVERTISING BEING REPLACED OR MERELY DISPLACED?

Political advertising is going through a shift that matches that of how the market consumes its information and media. It isn't so much as out with the old and in with the new but more using a method that allows for higher levels of effectiveness and engagement, at lower costs, with fast production times to enhance and match the dynamic nature of modern campaigning.

The personalisation of value exchanges on social media that are tied to issues that voters are engaged with, such as Climate Change or Brexit, has helped political advertising see a new dawn, turning voters from receivers of information to co-creators, often commenting, sharing and engaging with the media they view, the candidates they see and the parties that they vote for, such as that witnessed through the engagement with the Trump and Clinton brands in the 2016 US Presidential elections.

The support for this shift lies in the evidence from the market itself: although the value of political advertising across the world is increasing, media rates aside, the emergence of the citizen consumer turning from mere voter to being an active participant in the electoral process has significantly changed the use of political advertising and communications.

With the emergence of new paradigms in marketing, such as relationship marketing, services marketing and branding, there is some discussion by leading marketing theorists such as Vargo and Lusch (2004) or Grönroos (1994) that advertising may have a more minor role in the marketing campaigns of the future.

Before we get into why political advertising may be changing it is first necessary to understand some of the theory behind what makes advertising itself effective, and how political advertising draws on this theory in its application and development.

THE HOW, WHAT AND WHY BEHIND WHAT MAKES (POLITICAL) ADVERTISING WORK

Whilst political advertising is a unique subset of advertising itself (Lang 1991) to understand why political advertising may be effective, it is important to understand how advertising itself works.

Whilst there is no way under the sun that this can be accomplished in one chapter of this book, it is important to know what advertising is, and why it needs to evolve as new platforms, mediums, techniques and theory emerge in the current information age.

This section will start with a brief background on advertising, and then discuss how advertising is classified by type and purpose. It will then look at some general models of advertising response to understand what advertisers may be trying to achieve when they use different types of advertisements. This will help lay the foundations for a brief theoretical overview of political advertising.

First, to a brief background on advertising.

A Brief Background on Advertising

Advertising has been defined by the American Marketing Association (2013) as:

> *The placement of announcements and persuasive messages in time or space pur-*
> *chased in any of the mass media by business firms, nonprofit organizations,*
> *government agencies, and individuals who seek to inform and/or persuade*
> *members of a particular target market or audience about their products, ser-*
> *vices, organizations, or ideas.*

Rossiter and Bellman (2005) identify advertising as the most effective form of marketing communications used by an organisation to raise awareness of a product and achieve sales objectives. Advertising is used as part of a broader campaign to achieve communication objectives, such as increased levels of brand awareness, and to achieve sales objectives, such as market share.

The primary objectives of advertising are to inform consumers about new products and where they can purchase them, remind consumers to continue using certain products, persuade consumers to choose one brand over another, to reinforce and build relationships with customers and to assist the other elements of the marketing mix to achieve their objectives (Leiss et al. 2013).

Advertising's main strength is that it is the main medium used to reach a mass audience and the most effective vehicle to use to achieve communication objectives for a product, such as brand awareness, brand attitude and brand preference, and sales objectives (Petty et al. 1983). Its main weaknesses, although it has others, are the increasing negativity towards all forms of advertising, espeically in an online context, the cost to achieve reach and frequency targets, and the competing background of noise that can dilute the effectiveness of messages (Hoch and Ha 1986).

However, advertising comes in many different formats and types and it is important to know how to differentiate and classify advertising to gain a deeper knowledge of what makes it effective in certain contexts.

Classification of Advertising

Advertising can be classified into dynamic and static categories. Dynamic mass media advertising is constantly changing due to the electronic or interactive nature of the media and incorporates radio, television and internet advertising. Static mass media, which is in a permanent state and does not undergo any changes, includes print such as newspapers and magazines or static advertisements in movie cinemas, and outdoors such as billboards, transit stops or on roadways. Message duration is a distinguishing factor between the two formats as dynamic media is time constrained by design to deliver a changing message within a budget, content or broadcast requirement constraint. Static media is not bound by time in the sense that the message does not change during the course of observation and consumption.

Additional categories of advertising types have been identified in the literature by Rossiter and Bellman (2005) who proposed a three-part categorisation of advertising based on content addressing a brand, eliciting a direct response or furthering a specific corporate image in the mind of the consumers. Brand advertising aims to increase consumer awareness of a product-level brand through placement in many different types of mass media, where the message has the responsibility of providing information regarding the existence of the brand, and messages associated with the consumption of the branded product (Rossiter and Bellman 2005).

Direct-response advertising seeks to elicit a response to the message, such as information search, product trial or product purchase (Rossiter and Bellman 2005). In political marketing, this would equate to fundraising, calls for donations, pledges or membership drives. Corporate image advertising is designed to elicit positive attitudes towards the corporate or umbrella brand, rather than individual products, and can be undertaken to influence corporate reputation, repositioning or retail outlet selection (Rossiter and Bellman 2005). Political marketing has increasingly depended on a corporate image advertising style for leadership position, policy, attack adverts and party endorsements, although negative advertising is inconsistent with how this type of advertising works well, something practitioners should note.

General Models of Advertising Response

To understand why it is that advertising impacts upon the brand equity, or resonance, Keller (1993) discusses it is important to understand some models of consumer response to advertising stimuli.

Firstly, advertising influences consumers through communications effects. The Rossiter and Bellman (2005) version of the Holbrook and Batra (1987) model demonstrates how marketing communications has three simultaneous levels of effects on consumer responses. Consumers are assumed to move through a sequence of four steps in response to marketing communications (Greenwald and Leavitt 1984). Although presented as a linear sequence, these steps do not necessarily occur over a delayed period of time and may occur simultaneously once a consumer is exposed to a marketing communications message.

As a consumer is going through these steps, marketing communications is influencing them on three levels. Each level influences the others and, therefore, one level may be more important in influencing the action undertaken by the consumer as a consequence of being exposed to the message. For example, the emotion a consumer feels towards an advertisement will affect their purchase intent of a product and lead to action in the audience.

Furthermore the impact on emotional responses, from the first level processing affections on communication effects through to the decisions stages, is the focus here. Whilst Holbrook and Batra (1987) and Rossiter and Bellman (2005) have examined the impact of emotions on attitudes towards television advertising, and emotion on attitudes towards the brand, this book will expand on some of these points by examining the interaction between attention and emotions in the context of political brand communication effects.

All models of advertising work on the assumption that the viewer needs to be exposed to the message, and has to respond cognitively or emotionally to the message in order to be influenced by the message. This is why understanding what message arouses a viewer emotionally and in a way that they can encode and remember the message so that it changes their behaviour is important to understand.

One critical feature affects all models of advertising in a television context—how dynamic it is due to the construct of time. This means that a television advertisement due to its twin features of structure and content can present new information to be processed whenever this is different from the previous scene. How much information that is required to be processed is dependent upon how much new information is presented by the change in scene and structure.

This dynamic feature of television advertising is both a strength and weakness of this form of communication. This is a strength because information can be presented in such a way that the viewer can encode the message into their memory and then be persuaded to change their behaviour because of their emotional response to this message, sometimes without realising that this is what has happened. This is a weakness because presenting too much information and in the wrong way can prevent the message from being encoded and, therefore, fail in being encoded and remembered.

This weakness was first explored by Kahneman (1973) in his seminal book, *Attention and Effort*, which examined the relationship between the amount of information a person was exposed to and their attention to this information. Kahneman found that a person had a limited capacity for attention at any one time, but the capacity was variable depending upon several factors, including the stimulus and the person's involvement levels with the information they were being exposed to. In many ways Kahneman's (1973) work, which he extended into other areas of research, laid the foundation for much of the work in advertising relating to involvement with messages and attention to them.

This is reflected by research by Lang et al. (1999) and Lang (2000, 2006) into television advertising, which is relevant to this thesis as it explored the relationship between structural and content components and attention to a message. Lang (2000) and Lang et al. (1999) found that the more information a viewer was presented with, the more their limited capacity for attention would be used up. Once the capacity was reached then a viewer's attention levels would drop away dramatically and focus on secondary tasks not related to the primary stimulus they were being exposed to. In a practical sense this could mean, for example, going off to make a cup of tea whilst the television programme was still running or half way through a message break.

Due to the complex nature of predicting when this capacity might be reached it was easier for researchers, such as Lang, to understand how this capacity could be used up quickly. Lang found that certain structural features, such as pacing (the number of cuts in a message) and edits, were presenting new information to the viewer every time they occurred, using up the capacity for information processing of the viewer.

Lang also found that certain types of content could also use up this capacity due to the human body's response mechanism to stimulus, especially negative stimulus. This natural "fight or flight" response of the body to viewing negative stimulus means that it is given more processing resources than other stimulus, but it also means that for this reason that arousal is increased towards the message.

However, other elements of the message itself can also influence the processing of the message, such as message appeal type, for example, humour. A consumer's attitude towards the advertisement and sponsoring brand, and involvement with the product category is also important as it moderates involvement with the message and the information in it (Rossiter and Bellman 2005).

Political Marketing Communications and Political Advertising—Objectives

Political advertising has two main objectives—to make the target market aware of the value offering of the organisation and to influence the behaviour of the consumer so that they develop a liking and preference for that brand which then becomes an intention to purchase.

These broad objectives of advertising apply to Kaid's (2004) definition of political advertising as "a means through which parties and candidates present themselves to the electorate, mostly through the mass media". Kaid (2004) states the defining characteristics of political advertising are control of the message and use of mass communication channels to distribute the message, which is consistent with meeting the broad objectives of political advertising as explained earlier.

Whilst the role, characteristics and definition of political advertising point to the use of positive messaging to achieve communication objectives, this has not been the case in more recent times. Although nearly all political campaigns have used an element of negativity to attack the credibility of their opponents, it is only recently where this has started to accelerate in use to become the dominant method of communication in political campaigns (Ansolabehere and Iyengar 2010; Kaid 2012). This is despite the contradiction on what makes marketing effective which is implicit in its definition and its application through the promise of exchange, a point noted by Ansolabehere and Iyengar (2010) who argue that positive messaging can stimulate people to vote and instil confidence in the democratic system of government.

Despite these points, negative messaging is preferred for the perceived strategic effect it has by political organisations. These strategic effects of negative advertising can have a range of purposes. One might be to influence voter turnout by either turning voters off voting through increasing despondency and mistrust in the political process and, therefore, encouraging not voting in the election, or by increasing voter turnout through creating a fear of a political candidate or party being elected (Ansolabehere and Iyengar 2010; Kaid 1997, 2012; Merritt 1984).

Another purpose might be to increase the probability of influencing a desired action amongst the target market through a message of fear or anger (Ansolabehere and Iyengar 2010; Kaid 2012). More recent research from a political communications perspective by Fowler and Ridout (2013) on the 2012 US Presidential election states that the rise in negative advertising could be partly attributed to the perceived closeness of races by political organisations and the use of mainstream media to achieve communication objectives. It is this latter point, they argue, has created a need to obtain publicity through making aggressive negative messages that get the attention of the media.

This is reinforced by their finding that the dominant emotion portrayed in negative messages in the 2012 US Presidential race was anger, with 74% of all messages screened having this emotion somewhere in the advertisement (Fowler and Ridout 2013). The closest positive emotion was enthusiasm at 31% (Fowler and Ridout 2013). In the Australian Federal election of 2013, the losing Australian Labor Party had used 75% negative messages, but the winning Liberal Party had used 70% of positive messages (ebuqity.com 2013), which might indicate that political parties are seeing the positive light at the end of the negative tunnel.

Yet, contrasted with commercial marketing from an advertising perspective there are very few reasons why a negative message should work or be more successful than a positive one at creating arousal. Very few commercial campaigns ever use negative messages to achieve communication objectives, with perhaps the good example being the Energizer Duracell commercials that used a pink rabbit to highlight the advantages of one brand over the other.

The reason is clear from most advertising literature: the best ways to influence a consumer is to make them like a message so that they pay more attention to it, then store the message in their memory and hopefully influence their behaviour through purchase intention or brand preference. This is seen from models, such as the Rossiter and Bellman (2005) model, to the Petty et al. (1983) model of central and peripheral routes of persuasion—the best way to make a consumer like a message and pay attention to it is to use appeals that they will like to watch.

However, there is one final element to advertising that might explain the contrast in effects between positive and negative political advertising and commercial advertising—structural effects. Advertising comprises two main features: content or valence and structural effects. Whilst the content of the message, either positive or negative, can influence liking and emotional response to a message, this can be either emphasised more or less by the use of structural effects. Structural effects are techniques such as cuts, edits, zooms or length. These effects can also play a role in liking and attitudes towards the advertisement, although what exact role structural effects have on political advertising has not been thoroughly investigated, but the research in commercial advertising is enough to suggest that they can have a significant role (Lang 2000).

Political Advertising in Political
Marketing Campaigns—Characteristics

Political advertising has three unique characteristics that differentiate it from commercial marketing activity. First, political brands communicate exchanges of value and loss in the same campaign, which does not happen in commercial product marketing. This means that communication of exchanges will be in both positive (focusing on the promise of value) and negative (focusing on the promise of loss) to the market. Similar strategies do occur in social marketing, but these campaigns are usually built around singular brands that have long-term objectives, whereas political marketing exchanges of both value and loss focus on the duality concept (party and candidate) of political offerings.

Second, the whole of a nation's population will be part of a political marketing exchange, but only some will willingly purchase the product (e.g., vote for the government). Few, if any, other products have this level of impact on society. This means that, at every election, to effectively communicate a value of exchange to the market, political brands need to overcome existing attitudes towards the brand and advertisement that have been created around the brand in the previous term of government.

These attitudes will differ not only due to the perception of what brands should do in the government and what they should do in opposition but also due to attitudes towards political brands in general and also involvement with the political process and political stakeholders.

Third, political advertising is still primarily focused on shorter time frames, such as election campaigns that can last anywhere from one year to one month in duration, depending upon the political system, and where leader brands can be vastly different from election to election (Butler and Collins 1994; Hughes 2007, Needham 2005; O'Shaughnessy 2001; Strömbäck 2007).

This is in contrast with commercial marketing where campaigns are continuous and last for as long as the product does, communicating only promises of value using positive messaging. As advertising is the primary method of communication and creation of exchange in political marketing, other methods of integrated marketing communications, such as sales promotions and sponsorship, do not have the same degree of emphasis or use as in commercial marketing. These attributes, combined with attitudes towards the brand, leads to a need for political messages to create arousal towards their message and product in a shorter time frame than commercial marketing.

Political Advertising—Introduction

As in other forms of marketing, advertising is the single biggest expense of political marketing campaigns and this reason is primarily due to the use of television advertising to achieve communication objectives.

Kaid (2012) notes, political advertising continues to be the foundation of political marketing, both in the United States and the rest of the world regardless of the political system or culture. Political advertising has covered a wide range of communication platforms even from its early history, such as Atkin and Heald's (1976) study into the effects of radio and television political advertising on cognitive and affective orientations, Rothschild and Ray's (1974) study into how advertising affects involvement with politics, and Kaid and Sanders's (1978) investigation into how the type and length of political television commercials influenced consumers.

Research in political advertising has varied in motivation, methods and context ranging from understanding democratic effects, such as influencing voter turnout (Marcus et al. 2000), to understanding consumer behaviour by using methods, such as surveys to scientific methods such as psychophysiological measures, such as eye tracking, heart rate and skin conductance (Bradley et al. 2007; Hughes 2014, Lang 1991).

Research into dynamic types of political advertising has largely focused on the television advertising as the main method of influencing consumers of political products. Political advertising has been a dominant form of communication between politicians and the voting public (Kaid 1997). Political campaigns worldwide have historically emphasised television commercial (TVC) spend with up to 70% of political marketing campaigns focusing on TVC spend compared to an average of 35% for commercial campaigns (Miskin and Grant 2004).

Similarly, Miskin and Grant (2004) demonstrated the relatively low spend on static advertising at 20% in some campaigns with the remaining 10% split across the other advertising alternatives, such as print and radio (Miskin and Grant 2004). Television advertising spend in an election campaign has been estimated at 70% of the total spend (Miskin and Grant 2004).

Consumer attention of television advertising in election campaigns in Australia reinforced this point, with an average of 70% attention paid to television advertising on the five federal campaigns held during the period 1990–2001. Figures for newspaper advertising material averaged 60% and radio only 47% (Australian Electoral Studies as per Miskin and Grant 2004).

The 2012 US Presidential campaigns saw television advertising remaining as the dominant form of political communication, with figures over two-thirds of all media used.

Defining Political Advertising

Just as the domain of political marketing still is unsettled on key areas such as exchange, stakeholder classification and the political market, so is one of the key components of political marketing management: political advertising. Differences exist between practitioners and researchers, and even here differences among researchers and differences among practitioners. In Australia, for example, the main practitioner self-regulation organisation, the Advertising Standards Bureau, defines political advertising as:

> *Political advertising is advertising that attempts to influence or comment upon a matter which is currently the subject of extensive political debate. It includes advertising or marketing communications about a political party, representative or candidate, advertising about political issues or issues of public interest, and advertising in relation to government policies (whether published/broadcast by the government or someone else). Advertising by Government, political parties, lobby groups and other interest groups may fall into this category, and advertising may not just be during elections.* (2013)

Political advertising does not have a commonly accepted definition; however, commonality exists with regard to the focus on communication being paid and being political in nature. The most cited definition is by Kaid in the *Handbook of Political Communication* (2004: 154) who defines political advertising as being:

> any message primarily under the control of a source used to promote political candidates, parties, policy issues and/or ideas through mass channels.

Holtz-Bacha and Kaid (2006) updated this definition to take into consideration that political advertising does not just use mass channels, particularly in the era of the internet and social media (Kaid 2012). The updated definition is:

> a means through which parties and candidates present themselves to the electorate, mostly through the mass media. (Holtz-Bacha and Kaid 2006: 3)

These definitions have their foundations in both the political marketing and advertising literature. The American Marketing Association defines advertising as being:

The placement of announcements and persuasive messages in time or space purchased in any of the mass media by business firms, nonprofit organizations, government agencies, and individuals who seek to inform and/or persuade members of a particular target market or audience about their products, services, organizations, or ideas. (American Marketing Association 2013)

This definition has clear linkages to the definition of marketing, and also the central tenet of all marketing theory: the ability to communicate offerings of value to target markets to facilitate exchanges. Whilst the political advertising definitions of Kaid, and others, do not specifically mention the definition of advertising used by the AMA, it can be assumed that Kaid takes this definition into consideration when framing the definition of political advertising under the broader umbrella of marketing communications.

Televised Political Advertising

Televised political advertising has been defined as:

moving image programming that is designed to promote the interests of a given party or individual. (Kaid and Holtz-Bacha 1995: 2)

As political advertising uses communication channels to get the message to the market, its development as a method by political marketing managers is related to the development of media communication methods. This meant print was dominant in use in political advertising until the emergence of television as a mass communication method in the 1960s and 1970s. Television took over from newspapers as the most widely used method of political communications with the advent of colour television in the mid-late 1970s around the globe, and has remained there ever since.

Global figures on actual spend on televised political advertising are hard to ascertain, likely to be in hundreds of millions US dollars a year, although Plasser and Plasser (2002) provide a good summary of indicative costs in most countries of the world. Without any doubt the most expensive and probably the most intensive televised political advertising campaigns take place in the US Presidential elections, held every four years. The 2012 US Presidential election had an estimated three million television advertisements and cost at least US$2 billion (Fowler and Ridout 2013).

The current challenger to television advertising is the internet, more specifically social media. The emergence of the internet first started as internet penetration into homes began to reach over the 40–50% levels in most parts of the world by the late 1990s and early 2000s.

Despite, the emergence of Google and YouTube in 2007 and the emergence of smartphones that helped grow social media websites that compete for screen space, there are now multiple methods that a political campaigner can use to reach multiple markets simultaneously. In some cases, such as the Arab Spring Uprising (Shirky 2011) or the Euro Crisis (Stieglitz and Dang-Xuan 2013), this can be done more effectively than television, radio or print due to higher levels of engagement, involvement and interaction with the message and other stakeholders.

As a high visibility broadcast medium, television advertising has been favoured by political marketers and the political campaign industry. For example, in the 2012 US election, Mitt Romney's campaign in the Florida primary resulted in 13,000 television commercials across several networks to influence Republican voters at a multi-million dollar cost, which accounted for a larger proportion of the advertising spend than other platforms (The Washington Post 2012).

Types of Televised Political Advertising

Political advertising plays a dual role of ensuring that the public is aware of an opponent's weaknesses whilst promoting the sponsoring candidate's strengths and policy differences (O'Cass 2002; Pinkleton 1998; Meirick 2002; Roddy and Garramone 1988). Candidates can control the message sent to the target audience and its format, and can associate the sponsoring candidate with positive images and their opponent with negative images (Roddy and Garramone 1988; Christ et al. 1994; Niffenegger 1989).

As political products are usually associated with a personality, several researchers have suggested that the most effective means of highlighting differences between one political product and another is to use advertising that associates negative images with opposing candidates (Roddy and Garramone 1988; Lau et al. 1999; Pinkleton et al. 2002; Meirick 2002; James and Hensel 1991; Sorescu and Gelb 2000).

Political advertising uses both positive and negative campaign messaging. Although negative advertising is not unique to the political market, the use of negative "attack ads" on competing brands is far more widespread. Nearly all Western democratic elections have been dominated by the use of negative advertising media (Miskin and Grant 2004). In the 2012 Republican Presidential Nomination campaign, over 76% of television advertisements shown up until 6 March 2012 were negative (The Washington Post 2012). Although advertising is commonly applied in political marketing, limited research has examined the effect of political advertising upon a consumer's emotional engagement with the political brand, democratic processes and institutions.

EMOTIONS AND POLITICAL ADVERTISING

Emotions

Emotion has been defined in journal papers over 80 times (Scherer 2005), making it one of the most contested definitions in academia. Emotions are of interest to researchers in many areas due to their importance in the decision-making and analytical process by people. Nearly every single model of psychology, psychiatry, consumer behaviour, advertising, psychophysiology and communications has an emotional stage or focus. This is because of the importance emotions have in influencing and sometimes predicting human behaviour. Emotion can be defined as

> *an episode of interrelated, synchronized changes in the states of all or most of the five organismic subsystems in response to the evaluation of an external or internal stimulus event as relevant to major concerns of the organism.* (Scherer 2005)

The diversity of reactions that make up emotions can be divided into two types (Rossiter and Bellman 2005). The first category of emotions, type 1 emotions or lower order emotions, are spontaneous and uncontrollable reactions, such as pleasure and arousal. The second category of emotions, type 2 emotions or higher order emotions, require cognitive appraisal to recognise their existence. These are emotions such as love, desire, contempt and sadness (Poels and Dewitte 2006).

Attentional capacity is the information capacity a person has that is able to decode, process, encode and store information (Lang 1994). The capacity of any person is limited due to several factors (Lang 1994), but is mediated by their emotional response to a message. From a political marketing perspective, emotional arousal that leads to recall is of interest for delivering the political message.

To understand how the levels of emotions in television advertising change due to structure and content of the advertisement it is necessary to understand how the viewer watches the advertisement, how much attention they are giving to the message and when they stop paying attention in an environment as close as possible to how that occurs. Although this type of research is not new to the study of television or to the study of emotions, this approach has been used only once in the area of political advertising before to understand how viewers pay attention to and are aroused by television advertisements of political messages (Hughes 2014).

Does Political Advertising Generate Emotional Responses?

Political marketing research needs to, as Dann et al. (2007) said, "reignite the fire" by using more modern methods of marketing research to uncover new research findings and opportunities to help explain more deeply and fully how consumers interact with politics as a product.

As Lees-Marshment (2001) noted, political marketing is a marriage between politics and marketing, and therefore regardless if a party is a market- or marketing-oriented party when it comes to political advertising a party or candidate needs to generate an emotional response to generate action from the targeted stakeholders.

More recently, Harris and Sun (2017) noted that political marketing can be categorised into three key aspects: electoral, governmental and international contexts. In each of these the use of marketing is important in achieving outcomes, but as are other elements, such as public affairs, that also rely upon the generation of an emotional response to affect behaviour change and actions.

Whilst most political advertising research to date has examined the more strategic use of the method, there has been only a small amount of work done on how consumers might actually be responding emotionally to political television advertising.

Considering how important emotional response is in any model of advertising, understanding what makes a voter respond emotionally to an advertisement, or what structural or content aspect of a message arouses their levels of interest in a message, is important in understanding how political advertising can be effective.

Negative Advertising

Negative advertising can trace its history back to the early part of the twentieth century and has been frequently used as a campaign tool by political parties. Kaid (1997) noted that, during the 1980s, around 30% to 50% of all political advertisements during campaigns were negative; however, in 1992 and 1996 just under 70% of the advertisements in Bill Clinton's campaigns were negative. Despite this growth in the use of negative political advertising, some research have suggested it harms the democratic process (Faber et al. 1993; Garramone 1984; Roddy and Garramone 1988; Schenck-Hamlin et al. 2000; Jasperson and Fan 2002).

The factors present in negative political advertising vary according to the type of advertising appeal and message frame used. Using the definitions outlined above, the defining factors of a negative advertising campaign include:

- A negative message (Meirick 2002; Richardson 2001; Lau and Pomper 2001; Pinkleton 1997; Johnson-Cartee and Copeland 1991; Roddy and Garramone 1988).
- Paid advertising forming part of the overall communications strategy (Pinkleton 1997; Rossiter and Percy 1987).
- Advertising sponsored by one candidate who directs it at a political opponent (Bullock 1994; Haddock and Zanna 1997; Kaid 1997; Shapiro and Rieger 1992; Hill 1989).
- A typically comparative approach (Shapiro and Rieger 1992; Pinkleton 1998; James and Hensel 1991).
- A focus on issues and image, rather than policy (Pinkleton 1997; Kaid et al. 1992a; Johnson-Cartee and Copeland 1989).
- An emphasis on a certain target audience during a campaign (King et al. 1998).
- Specific attention to a particular image or issue that a candidate is associated with (King et al. 1998).

Based on the above characteristics, a new definition of negative political advertising can be defined as:

Advertising that targets the attacked candidate's weakness in issues or image and that highlights the sponsoring candidate's strengths in these areas by sending a negatively framed message.

A gap in the political marketing literature exists with regard to the effectiveness of negative advertising. As negative advertising is currently the dominant advertising method within political campaigns, presumptions of success have carried the approach from one campaign to the next. This raises a question of whether communicating a promise of loss is more effective than communicating a promise of value. Although research has questioned the efficacy of negative advertising, such as Bradley et al. (2007), studies using psychophysiological methods produced a finding that negative advertising may not be as effective.

These studies, even though few in number, are indicating that whilst negative advertisements are able to generate recall about the advertisement and the brand, they are not generating arousal that may be indicative of a negative or impartial attitude towards the advertisement, brand or both. However, as these studies can only examine a small number of message content and structure variables there is more research required to confirm these findings.

The important item of note here is that most studies into negative advertising have found that there is a relationship between negative advertising and recall. However, very few of these studies have been on the content of negative advertising, not what the relationship is between content and structure in an advertisement, so the cause of this relationship needs to be examined further in a more scientific aspect.

Whilst the political marketing literature defines negative advertising on the above criteria, negative advertising is seen slightly differently by those in communication research. Whether or not a message is defined as negative is far broader, and does not only consider whether or not the message is attacking another person or organisation. Images alone can make an advertisement negative in communication theory. For example, an advertisement for a horror movie will be defined as negative as the images are negative in content that leads to an increase in arousal by the viewer (Cacioppo et al. 2007).

Verbal elements of the message can also make a message negative. For example, an advertisement that has an unhappy voice-over for an overseas aid organisation, even if the image itself is not unhappy or unpleasant, may be defined as negative due to the verbal content that is negative in the message (Cacioppo et al. 2007). Then there are the structural elements that can influence how the viewer perceives an advertisement. These are elements such as cuts, edits, zooms, lighting, sound (volume, type and length) and time of the message itself. All of these can be used in a way that can make a message appear either negative or positive, which will now be discussed in further detail.

The Relationship Between Memory, Recall and Negative Political Advertising

Lang (2000) noted that every person only has a limited capacity for message processing. Therefore, being able to recall details of a message in this environment means that the message is deemed effective. Achieving recall of the negative advertisement and brand would indicate that the viewer paid attention to the message. This makes political communications unique as they are one of the very few areas where consumers are exposed to both messages that communicate exchange offerings of loss and value, with the expectation that they will remember details of each. As a strategy, this can work in several ways. For example, messages of loss may try and strengthen the promise of value by raising doubt over the offering of the attacked brand, or by creating doubt of the existing value offering of a preferred party or candidate. Recall has been linked to brand familiarity (Baker et al. 1986).

The more familiar a respondent is with a brand the more likely they are to recall attributes of a message from that brand, even if that message is new (Kent and Allen 1994). This would suggest that maximising recall of a message and the brand is an important metric for political marketers. However, political marketers may not fully understand how this works in practice.

This new area sees studies in communications and psychophysiology as helping understand this relationship from a more scientific perspective. Cacioppo et al. (2007) note several studies where there is a higher emotional response to negative images or scenes (e.g., war, forests being cut down) due to humans having a startle response or, as it is more commonly known as, a flight or fight response.

As the body is designed to prioritise attention to these images over everything else, this leads to higher recall for these images and scenes (Lang et al. 1993; Nabi 1999). Positive scenes do not have the same arousal and thus recall potential unless they are linked to a positive life experience (Miller et al. 2002).

New Frontiers in Learning and Evidence: Psychophysiological Measurement in Political Advertising

Psychophysiological Measures of Advertising

Psychophysiological techniques are used to understand how a viewer is aroused emotionally by a stimulus, and have been applied political advertising by Bradley et al. (2007). However, as television advertisement comprises two elements (structure and content) any research in this area can only take an incremental approach, as the use of psychophysiological methods is restricted to only one or two variables at a time.

Consequently, this incremental approach requires researchers to sequentially narrow the gaps of knowledge to areas or relationships that are impacting upon the effectiveness of political advertising. Knowing how consumers emotionally respond to the duality concept of political exchange that is currently offered by political brands is also important in understanding the effectiveness of not just political advertising but also political marketing.

Psychophysiological measurement allows for phenomenological issues in communications and advertising to be better understood in the context in which they occur. This is both in the mind of the respondent and the environment in which the viewing may occur.

As such, this area of research is growing rapidly as researchers recognise the advantages of being able to capture the measurement and meaning of the cognitive and emotional processing of media, extending knowledge and understanding of the unique phenomenological aspects of marketing and communications when used in practice. Prior studies on the effects of political advertising on consumers have used methodologies that have not measured the psychophysiological responses of respondents to the material they have viewed.

Attention is important in understanding how a viewer's memory, physiology and behaviour are being affected by the medium (Lang 1990). There are two main areas of attention research in advertising: intermedia—advertising across different types of mediums—and intramedia—advertising within the one medium (Lang 1990). Intermedia is concerned primarily with tonic responses which are long-term responses that reflect a viewer's decision to attend to specific programme or medium.

Intramedia is concerned primarily with a viewer's phasic responses, which are short-term responses that reflect brief changes in the level of attention of a viewer during a single media presentation (Lang 1990) so research in political advertising on television and video in the future needs to consider using a more appropriate intramedia methodology that will examine a viewer's phasic response to televised political advertisements.

Relationship Between the Psychophysiological Processing of Media and Memory

Memory recall of political advertising content is a key aim of political advertising. As memory recall is associated with learning and attention, it is influential in the brand communication effects that are recognised as critical influencers on the consumer decision-making process (Rossiter and Bellman 2005). There are three main ways to measure recall, each related to a separate part of memory processing. Recognition recall measures how well a message was encoded. Cued recall measures how well a message was stored. Free recall measures how easily the message is accessed from memory (Potter and Bolls 2012).

The more arousing a message, the more likely that this message will be transferred into the memory of the viewer (Lang 2000, 2006). Therefore, this would tend to suggest that using negative scenes and images would help recall of information in an advertisement. This theory has been applied to social marketing, which is similar to political marketing, where negative images are used in messages to increase arousal to, and memory for, the message.

Social marketing studies have examined the link between the use in social marketing communications of negative images and attitudes and arousal to messages. Hastings et al. (2004) found that using negative images in messages may make them more memorable, but also contributed negative attitudes towards the advertisement and the sponsoring brand. This made it more difficult for the campaign to achieve long-term objectives as target markets were not paying attention to the message to make it effective due to their attitudes towards it and secondary markets were developing a higher threshold level that would require new communication campaigns to be planned (Hastings et al. 2004).

Lang's (2006) paper on designing an effective cancer campaign message considered the use of negative content and how this could be used to positively influence attention and memory levels of viewers. Whilst there was a likelihood of negative content creating a negative attitude towards the advertisement, it was also theorised that, to some viewers, the negative content may act as a motivator and influence their behaviour. Arousal could be further enhanced by the use of structural features that elicited higher levels of arousal and emotional response from viewers.

In political advertising, earlier studies have indicated that negative advertisements generate higher recall than positive advertisements (Roberts 1995; Shapiro and Rieger 1992; Lang 1991; Merritt 1984). In contrast, other political marketing research has drawn the opposite con- clusion (Kaid et al. 1992a, b). More recently Bradley et al. (2007) have found higher recall of negative political advertising than positive messaging.

The effect of each type of advertisement can be contrasted with levels of consumer brand preference, attitude and recall to determine what type of televised advertisement has the greatest impact on consumers in a polit- ical context. This can identify the objectives, features and types of televised political advertising. The amount of information contained in each adver- tisement has been identified (Lang 1991) as an important factor in increas- ing the level of emotion in a consumer. As a result of the literature, it is projected that negative advertisements, with their greater cognitive com- mitments, will result in higher levels of recall than demonstrated by posi- tive advertising, which is supported by the works of Rossiter and Bellman (2005), Lang (1991), Brians and Wattenberg (1996) Roberts (1995) Shapiro and Rieger (1992) Lang (1991), Lemert et al. (1999), and Merritt (1984).

Phasic Responses and Attention Orientation

Lang (1990) identified three basic mechanisms of phasic attention change: orienting response (OR), startle response (SR) and defensive response (DR). Lang (1990) and Reeves et al. (1985) suggest that orientating response is the mechanism by which phasic attention varies in response to the structural features of television advertising as viewers use these features to orientate their focus of attention in a dynamic environment.

Another effect of structural features of television is that they can elicit orienting responses in attentive viewers causing variation of attention lev- els within a viewing session. These orienting responses increase recall for information immediately following the OR eliciting structural feature. It is this effect that supports the theory of how structural features of television can guide viewers' attention (Lang 1990; Singh and Rothschild 1983).

Reeves et al. (1985) also found evidence to support the proposition that structural features influence learning through the mechanism of an orienting response. Reeves found significant correlation between atten- tion to structural features and recall for information immediately follow- ing the attention-capturing structural feature. This would support the hypothesis that duration of attention to structural features can help increase recall of the message and of the brand itself. Therefore, it can be

theorised that, as ORs are part of a phasic response towards an advertisement, a recall of information in the message would help a political campaign that has only a short duration.

Orienting Response and Structural Features

Structural features of a television advertisement are those features that are
not content related (Lang 1990). They can include commercial onset,
movements, zooms, cuts and edits (Lang 1990). Categorisation of a television advertisement can be done across each of these structural features
so that they can be examined together or as separate variables.

Orienting responses are elicited by a change in the environment (Lang
1990). In television, this means a stimulus, such as a structural feature that
can change the viewing environment and lead to a change in orienting
response (Lang 1990). A structural change can also cue to the viewer that
the viewing environment has just changed (Lang 1990). Television can
achieve a change in orienting response by signal and by novel characteristics. Novel structural features can be features, such as an edit, cut, zoom
or music onset or points of interest, such as an item in the message like a
car (Lang 1990). Each point of interest needs to be at least 6 seconds apart
in order to measure a cardiac-orienting response (Lang 1990).

Arousal

Arousal is influenced by structural features and content of television.
Arousal levels may vary briefly in response to a stimulus or arousal levels
may increase or decrease consistently over a long period of time.
Physiological arousal is measured by phasic changes reflected in oscilla-
tions of the level of arousal around a consistent baseline.

Arousal has been found to influence subsequent learning (Lang 1990).
Arousal was thought to be a unitary concept, but is now seen as measured
across multiple constructs and dimensions. Researchers vary on how it can
be measured, having either two dimensions (physiological and cognitive) or
three dimensions (behavioural, physiological and cognitive) (Lang 1990).

Physiological dimensions are the dimensions best measured in relation
to television advertising due to their ease of measurement. Arousal can be
influenced by levels of emotion in the content of television being viewed
(Lang 1991). Research on emotion consistently reduces the lists of feelings to two or three stable dimensions: direction, control and arousal. As

the processing of emotions contains a component of physiological arousal it is logical to suggest that emotional content in television should result in increased physiological arousal (Lang 1990, Potter and Bolls 2012).

Interaction of Attention and Arousal

Kahneman (1973) argued that a relationship exists between a person's level of arousal and the level of attention or cognitive capacity that a person has available to process a stimulus. He argued that as arousal increases so does attention. Applying that to television it could be argued that an aroused viewer will have a higher level of attention than a non-aroused viewer.

Emotion can increase attention to a message. Emotional responses to advertising stimulus improve memory by increasing arousal, which then increases cognitive capacity (Kahneman 1973; Thorson et al. 1985). Consequently, there should be an interaction between the effects of televised emotions and the effects of structural features on attention and arousal because any increase in arousal should result in an increase in phasic attention corresponding to a more vigorous orienting response.

Therefore, the more emotional that the viewer finds an advertisement, the greater that they will be aroused by that advertisement. This increases attention to the advertisement and, therefore, recall for information. As arousal is a phasic response, this can be measured by skin conductance. Consequently, with regard to the combination of arousal and message recall, it would be expected that advertising with higher levels of arousal would have greater levels of recall.

Is It Time to Stop Political Advertising?

Current Research Findings Using Psychophysiological Methods

Psychophysiological theory considers the content and formal elements as being important in deciding if the advertisement is negative or positive, rather than who the message might be targeted at or about. This method is the preferred one to analyse commercials as prior studies that have used negative and positive valence as variables in studies have found significant differences in how respondents view, attend and remember each. The important difference between psychophysiological communication theory and political marketing theory in this area is that the psychophysiological theory takes a bottom-up perspective whereas the political marketing literature takes a more top-down approach.

The other significant feature of this methodology over existing ones is that it allows for the real-time measurement and collection of data in an environment that closely replicates that in which a participant would watch television at home. There have also been studies, although none yet in politics, that track and measure how participants use apps on mobile devices in real time, which is perhaps the next frontier for political advertising research.

Early psychophysiological studies in politics (Bradley et al. 2007), which investigated negative political advertising, found mixed results for the emotional level of intensity elicited from participants. However, no study to date has included the ads in a television programme which replicates how a participant would watch television, including environmental conditions such as a lounge room with a recliner, and then captured those responses in real time using psychophysiological methods.

That is until Hughes (2014) undertook a study at the Interactive Television Research Institute in Perth, Western Australia, that did exactly this. This study consisted of using psychophysiological measures and a post-test survey to examine respondents' emotional responses to televised political advertisements that varied by a structural feature that could influence arousal (pace) and valence (negative/positive).

This study investigated the effect of pacing and valence on responses to political advertisements. The viewing session consisted of six programme segments of 7 minutes long, each of a pre-recorded PG popular rated television show and five ad breaks. The first four ad breaks featured 30-second commercials and these were separated by 30-second filler advertisements.

Although advertisement type order was fixed (filler, test, filler, test, filler, test, filler) all placement allocations for each advertisement type were randomly allocated to avoid order effects. The advertisements in Ad Break Five were fixed and not used as test advertisements. The political advertisements were categorised into party (Australian Labor Party/Liberal Party), pace of advertisement (slow, medium, fast), and whether the advertisement was negative or positive. Coding of the advertisements was based on a prior study and using a small cohort of non-participants to act as verification and validation of these results.

As all participants saw all advertisements, a within subjects design was used that compared the responses to the different types of political advertisements. Additionally, to test the response to a competing preferred political party advertisement, a between-groups analysis was also conducted. A total of 69 participants who met the criteria of being stimulant free were used for the study, and were representative of the Australian population based on age. Data was analysed using the within subjects approach of the repeated measures ANOVA with a Huynh-Feldt epsilon correction when the assumption of sphericity was violated.

The results found overall that there was no difference in absolute skin conductance during the political advertisements regardless of voter preference for each party when compared to the resting baseline but there was a difference in arousals for the valence of the advertisements. These were significant findings as they were found under conditions as close to what a consumer would watch television in. In particular, that positive advertisements elicited higher emotional responses than negative advertisements was a finding that should act as a warning sign for those still putting their faith in methods that may have once worked but are now questionable at best. Whilst short-term recall tests indicated nearly equal findings for negative and positive advertising, the best medium- to long-term recalled advertisement by a significant margin was a Greens positive advertisement.

Another interesting finding from this study was that the post-test study found that 93% of participants expressed strong emotions against negative political advertising. So even though participants could recall an advertisement they did so because of their level of anger and hatred towards this form of advertising. No positive advertisement was recalled by participants and over half of participants reported feeling strong negative emotions towards the two largest parties for exposing them to negative advertising.

Whilst it should be noted that these results are yet to be replicated, they were done at a world-leading experimental laboratory and did replicate as close as possible the environment in which a consumer would actually watch television. Other evidence from practice indicates that these results are not inconsistent with what most people feel in relation to negative advertising. For example, an Australian Broadcasting Corporation Sydney Facebook study during the 2016 Australian election showed that over 83% of respondents hated negative advertising.

This evidence reveals the very smart reasons why commercial brands rarely venture into using negative advertising. Doing so leads to consumers switching off the advertisement they are watching, developing a deeper dislike of that form of advertising and far more importantly when it comes to behaviours, a deeper dislike of the brands that use them. Yes consumers recall information in the advertisements but there is no credibility attached to that information due to the level of anger and hatred they have for watching these types of advertisements.

This leaves the path open for brands and advertisements that don't use negative advertising or communications to gain consumer support rapidly and reinforce a positive message platform such as one built around a theme of change or hope. But it also raises questions of the harm being done to brand democracy of these types of advertisements, and the accidental exposure of future generations to these advertisements that then create pre-existing negative attitudes towards any form of political advertising and the brands that rely upon it.

As for political market orientation and political marketing orientation that can be forgotten, if parties are using advertising that is found to be offensive, by nearly all of the voting population. However, a brand that does consider the needs of the market in policy formulation, response to issues, engagement through relationship and the use of positive messaging to communicate value offerings is going to be successful either electorally or in connecting with stakeholders.

CONCLUSION

Political advertising is at the beginning of the end of one era and the start of a new one whose frontiers are yet to be fully explored by practitioners or researchers. Whilst traditional media still dominates practice, as the market evolves new media will slowly replace the role and use of traditional media types. Yet political advertising has also started to embark on a journey that may yet be its greatest of all and revolutionise politics and political campaigning: the increased use of positive advertisements in campaigns.

Consumers are tired of one-directional hate-filled messages in an era of politics that many have noted is one of the most vitriolic in human history. But this is the age of experiential marketing, relationship marketing and aspirational campaigns. An age typified by a fundamental change in how information is used and consumed. It will be this transformation of information due to digital technology and media, and the need to replace unengaging hate-filled messages with advertisements with those that promote value gains and experiences from a relationship with a brand, that will see the biggest innovations and fundamental changes in the future of political advertising in the years ahead.

REFERENCES

American Marketing Association. (2013). Definition of marketing. Retrieved July 15, 2013, from http://www.marketingpower.com/AboutAMA/Pages/DefinitionofMarketing.aspx

Ansolabehere, S., & Iyengar, S. (2010). *Going negative: How political advertisements shrink and polarize the electorate*. New York, NY: Simon and Schuster Inc.

Atkin, C., & Heald, G. (1976). Effects of political advertising. *Public Opinion Quarterly, 40*(2), 216–228.

Baker, W., Wesley Hutchinson, J., Moore, D., & Nedungadi, P. (1986). Brand familiarity and advertising: Effects on the evoked set and brand preference. *Advances in Consumer Research, 13*(1), 637–642.

Bradley, S. D., Angelini, J. R., & Lee, S. (2007). Psychophysiological and memory effects of negative political ads: Aversive, arousing, and well remembered. *Journal of Advertising, 36*(4), 115–127.

Brians, C. L., & Wattenberg, M. P. (1996). Campaign issue knowledge and salience: Comparing reception from TV commercials, TV news and newspapers. *American Journal of Political Science, 40*(1), 172–193.

Bullock, D. A. (1994). *The influence of political attack advertising on undecided voters: An experimental study of campaign message strategy*. PhD Thesis, University of Arizona.

Butler, P., & Collins, N. (1994). Political marketing: Structure and process. *European Journal of Marketing, 28*(1), 19–34.

Cacioppo, J. T., Tassinary, L. G., & Berntson, G. (2007). *Handbook of psychophysiology*. Cambridge: Cambridge University Press.

Christ, W. G., Thorson, E., & Caywood, C. (1994). Do attitudes toward political advertising affect information processing of televised political commercials? *Journal of Broadcasting & Electronic Media, 38*(3), 251–270.

Dann, S., Harris, P., Mort, G. S., Fry, M.-L., & Binney, W. (2007). Reigniting the fire: A contemporary research agenda for social, political and nonprofit marketing. *Journal of Public Affairs, 7*(3), 291–304.

Faber, R. J., Tims, A. R., & Schmitt, K. G. (1993). Negative political advertising and voting intent: The role of involvement and alternative information sources. *Journal of Advertising, 22*(4), 67–76.

Fowler, E. F., & Ridout, T. N. (2013). Negative, angry, and ubiquitous: Political advertising in 2012. *The Forum, 10*(4), 51–61.

Garramone, G. M. (1984). Voter responses to negative political ads. *Journalism and Mass Communication Quarterly, 61*(2), 250–259.

Greenwald, A. G., & Leavitt, C. (1984). Audience involvement in advertising: Four levels. *Journal of Consumer Research, 11*(1), 581–592.

Grönroos, C. (1994). Quo vadis, marketing? Toward a relationship marketing paradigm. *Journal of Marketing Management, 10*(5), 347–360.

Haddock, G., & Zanna, M. P. (1997). Impact of negative advertising on evaluations of political candidates: The 1993 Canadian federal election. *Basic and Applied Social Psychology, 19*(2), 205–223.

Harris, P., & Sun, H. (2017). The ends justify the means: A global research agenda for political marketing and public affairs. *Journal of Public Affairs, 17*(4).

Hastings, G., Stead, M., & Webb, J. (2004). Fear appeals in social marketing: Strategic and ethical reasons for concern. *Psychology & Marketing, 21*(11), 961–986.

Hill, R. P. (1989). An exploration of voter responses to political advertisements. *Journal of Advertising, 18*(4), 14–22.

Hoch, S. J., & Ha, Y.-W. (1986). Consumer learning: Advertising and the ambiguity of product experience. *Journal of Consumer Research, 13*(2), 221–233.

Holbrook, M. B., & Batra, R. (1987). Assessing the role of emotions as mediators of consumer responses to advertising. *Journal of Consumer Research, 14*(3), 404–420.

Holtz-Bacha, C., & Kaid, L. L. (2006). Political advertising in international comparison. In *The sage handbook of political advertising* (pp. 3–14).

Hughes, A. (2007). Personal brands: An exploratory analysis of personal brands in Australian political marketing. In *Australia and New Zealand Marketing Academy Conference*, 3–5 December, University of Otago, Dunedin, New Zealand.

Hughes, A. (2014). *The relationship between advertisement content and pacing on emotional responses and memory for televised political advertisements.* Doctoral thesis, The Australian National University.

James, K. E., & Hensel, P. J. (1991). Negative advertising: The malicious strain of comparative advertising. *Journal of Advertising, 20*(2), 53–69.

Jasperson, A. E., & Fan, D. P. (2002). An aggregate examination of the backlash effect in political advertising: The case of the 1996 US Senate race in Minnesota. *Journal of Advertising, 31*(1), 1–12.

Johnson-Cartee, K. S., & Copeland, G. A. (1989). Southern voters' reaction to negative political ads in 1986 election. *Journalism & Mass Communication Quarterly, 66*(4), 888–986.

Johnson-Cartee, K. S., & Copeland, G. A. (1991). *Negative political advertising: Coming of age.* Hillsdale, NJ: Routledge.

Kahneman, D. (1973). *Attention and effort.* Englewood Cliffs, NJ: Prentice Hall.

Kaid, L. L. (1997). Effects of the television spots on images of Dole and Clinton. *American Behavioral Scientist, 40*(8), 1085–1094.

Kaid, L. L. (2004). *Handbook of political communication research.* Mahwah, NJ: Lawrence Erlbaum Associates.

Kaid, L. L. (2012). Political advertising as political marketing: A retro-forward perspective. *Journal of Political Marketing, 11*(1–2), 29–53.

Kaid, L. L., & Holtz-Bacha, C. (1995). *Political advertising across cultures: Comparing content, styles, and effects. Political advertising in western democracies* (pp. 206–227). Thousand Oaks; London; New Delhi: Sage Publications.

Kaid, L. L., Chanslor, M., & Hovind, M. (1992a). The influence of program and commercial type on political advertising effectiveness. *Journal of Broadcasting & Electronic Media, 36*(3), 303–320.

Kaid, L. L., Leland, C. M., & Whitney, S. (1992b). The impact of televised political ads: Evoking viewer responses in the 1988 presidential campaign. *Southern Communication Journal, 57*(4), 285–295.

Keller, K. L. (1993). Conceptualizing, measuring, and managing customer-based brand. *Journal of Marketing, 57*, 1–22.

Kent, R. J., & Allen, C. T. (1994). Competitive interference effects in consumer memory for advertising: The role of brand familiarity. *The Journal of Marketing, 58*(3), 97–105.

King, E., Henderson, R., & Chen, H. (1998). Viewer response to positive vs negative ads in the 1996 presidential campaign. In *Annual meeting of the Midwest Political Science Association*, Chicago, 23–25 April.

Lang, A. (1990). Involuntary attention and physiological arousal evoked by structural features and emotional content in TV commercials. *Communication Research, 17*(3), 275–299.

Lang, A. (1991). Emotion, formal features, and memory for televised political advertisements. *Television and Political Advertising, 1*, 221–243.

Lang, A. (1994). Categorical and dimensional theories of emotion: How they predict memory for television messages. In *Annual meeting of the Association of Education in Journalism and Mass Communication*, Atlanta, GA, 10–13 August.

Lang, A. (2000). The limited capacity model of mediated message processing. *Journal of Communication, 50*(1), 46–70.

Lang, A. (2006). Using the limited capacity model of motivated mediated message processing to design effective cancer communication messages. *Journal of Communication, 56*(s1), S57–S80.

Lang, A., Bolls, P., Potter, R. F., & Kawahara, K. (1999). The effects of production pacing and arousing content on the information processing of television messages. *Journal of Broadcasting and Electronic Media, 43*(4), 451–475.

Lang, A., Geiger, S., Strickwerda, M., & Sumner, J. (1993). The effects of related and unrelated cuts on television viewers' attention, processing capacity, and memory. *Communication Research, 20*(1), 4–29.

Lau, R. R., & Pomper, G. M. (2001). Effects of negative campaigning on turnout in US Senate elections, 1988–1998. *Journal of Politics, 63*(3), 804–819.

Lau, R. R., Sigelman, L., Heldman, C., & Babbitt, P. (1999). The effects of negative political advertisements: A meta-analytic assessment. *American Political Science Review, 93*(4), 851–875.

Lees-Marshment, J. (2001). The marriage of politics and marketing. *Political Studies, 49*(4), 692–713.

Leiss, W., Kline, S., Jhally, S., & Botterill, J. (2013). *Social communication in advertising: Consumption in the mediated marketplace.* Routledge.

Lemert, J. B., Wanta, W., & Lee, T.-T. (1999). Party identification and negative advertising in a US Senate election. *Journal of Communication, 49*(2), 123–134.

Marcus, G. E., Russell Neuman, W., & MacKuen, M. (2000). *Affective intelligence and political judgment.* Chicago: University of Chicago Press.

Meirick, P. (2002). Cognitive responses to negative and comparative political advertising. *Journal of Advertising, 31*(1), 49–62.

Merritt, S. (1984). Negative political advertising: Some empirical findings. *Journal of Advertising, 13*(3), 27–38.

Miller, M. W., Patrick, C. J., & Levenston, G. K. (2002). Affective imagery and the startle response: Probing mechanisms of modulation during pleasant scenes, personal experiences, and discrete negative emotions. *Psychophysiology, 39*(4), 519–529.

Miskin, S., & Grant, R. (2004). *Political advertising in Australia.* Department of the Parliamentary Services.

Nabi, R. L. (1999). A cognitive-functional model for the effects of discrete negative emotions on information processing, attitude change, and recall. *Communication Theory, 9*(3), 292–320.

Needham, C. (2005). Brand leaders: Clinton, Blair and the limitations of the permanent campaign. *Political Studies, 53*(2), 343–361.

Niffenegger, P. B. (1989). Strategies for success from the political marketers. *Journal of Consumer Marketing, 6*(1), 45–51.

O'Cass, A. (2002). Political advertising believability and information source value during elections. *Journal of Advertising, 31*(1), 63–74.

O'Shaughnessy, N. (2001). The marketing of political marketing. *European Journal of Marketing, 35*(9/10), 1047–1057.

Petty, R. E., Cacioppo, J. T., & Schumann, D. (1983). Central and peripheral routes to advertising effectiveness: The moderating role of involvement. *Journal of Consumer Research, 10*(2), 135.

Pinkleton, B. (1997). The effects of negative comparative political advertising on candidate evaluations and advertising evaluations: An exploration. *Journal of Advertising, 26*(1), 19–29.

Pinkleton, B. E. (1998). Effects of print comparative political advertising on political decision-making and participation. *Journal of Communication, 48*(4), 24–36.

Pinkleton, B. E., Um, N.-H., & Austin, E. W. (2002). An exploration of the effects of negative political advertising on political decision making. *Journal of Advertising, 31*(1), 13–25.

Plasser, F., & Plasser, G. (2002). *Global political campaigning: A worldwide analysis of campaign professionals and their practices.* Portsmouth: Greenwood Publishing Group.

Poels, K., & Dewitte, S. (2006). *How to capture the heart? Reviewing 20 years of emotion measurement in advertising.* Department of Marketing and Organisation studies, Faculty of Economics and Applied Economics. Belgium: Catholic University of Leuven.

Potter, R. F., & Bolls, P. (2012). *Psychophysiological measurement and meaning: Cognitive and emotional processing of media.* New York, NY: Routledge.

Reeves, B. R., Thorson, E., Rothschild, M. L., McDonald, D., Hirsch, J., & Goldstein, R. (1985). Attention to television: Intrastimulus effects of movement and scene changes on alpha variation over time. *International Journal of Neuroscience, 27*(3–4), 241–255.

Roberts, M. S. (1995). Political advertising. In *Presidential campaign discourse: Strategic communication problems* (pp. 179–199).

Roddy, B. L., & Garramone, G. M. (1988). Appeals and strategies of negative political advertising. *Journal of Broadcasting & Electronic Media, 32*(4), 415–427.

Rossiter, J. R., & Bellman, S. (2005). *Marketing communications: Theory and applications*. Pearson/Prentice Hall.

Rossiter, J. R., & Percy, L. (1987). *Advertising and promotion management*. McGraw-Hill Book Company.

Rothschild, M. L., & Ray, M. L. (1974). Involvement and political advertising effect: An exploratory experiment. *Communication Research, 1*(3), 264–285.

Schenck-Hamlin, W. J., Procter, D. E., & Rumsey, D. J. (2000). The influence of negative advertising frames on political cynicism and politician accountability. *Human Communication Research, 26*(1), 53–74.

Scherer, K. R. (2005). What are emotions? And how can they be measured? *Social Science Information, 44*(4), 695–729.

Shapiro, M. A., & Rieger, R. H. (1992). Comparing positive and negative political advertising on radio. *Journalism & Mass Communication Quarterly, 69*(1), 135–145.

Shirky, C. (2011). The political power of social media-technology: The public sphere, and political change. *Foreign Affairs, 90*(1), 28–41.

Singh, S. N., & Rothschild, M. L. (1983). Recognition as a measure of learning from television commercials. *Journal of Marketing Research, 20*, 235–248.

Sorescu, A. B., & Gelb, B. D. (2000). Negative comparative advertising: Evidence favoring fine-tuning. *Journal of Advertising, 29*(4), 25–40.

Stieglitz, S., & Dang-Xuan, L. (2013). Social media and political communication: A social media analytics framework. *Social Network Analysis and Mining, 3*(4), 1277–1291.

Strömbäck, J. (2007). Antecedents of political market orientation in Britain and Sweden: Analysis and future research propositions. *Journal of Public Affairs, 7*(1), 79–89.

The Washington Post. (2012). Mad money: TV ads in the 2012 presidential campaign. Retrieved October 8, 2013, from http://www.washingtonpost.com/wp-srv/special/politics/track-presidential-campaign-ads-2012/

Thorson, E., Reeves, B., & Schleuder, J. (1985). Message complexity and attention to television. *Communication Research, 12*(4), 427–454.

Vargo, S. L., & Lusch, R. F. (2004). Evolving to a new dominant logic for marketing. *Journal of Marketing, 68*(1), 1–17.

CHAPTER 4

Weapons of Mass Consumption: Social and Digital Media in Political Campaigns

Abstract Social media is the latest and by far the most effective weapon of mass communication and it has been quickly adopted by political parties all around the world. This chapter delves into how digital and social media has been adopted and modified to be used as a campaign and relationship building strategy. The use of apps, such as Facebook, YouTube, Twitter, in moving voters from passive to active stakeholders will be examined.

There is also a discussion on how the use of database applications, such as NationBuilder, and data analytic firms, such as Cambridge Analytica, is transforming political campaigning and advertising by enabling parties and candidates of all sizes to be able to transform raw data from social media and mobile platforms into information on strategy, voters and advertising.

Keywords Facebook • Twitter • YouTube • Social media • Voter

IMAGERY AND SOCIAL MEDIA—MOVING THE VOTER CONSUMER FROM PASSIVE TO ACTIVE STAKEHOLDER

The continuous rise of social media as an influential source of information for consumers has been noted in everything from online travel forums (Xiang and Gretzel 2010) to customer satisfaction and decision making (Sashi 2012), music (Bu et al. 2010), through to social marketing cam-

© The Author(s) 2018   61
A. Hughes, *Market Driven Political Advertising*,
Palgrave Studies in Political Marketing and Management,
https://doi.org/10.1007/978-3-319-77730-6_4

paigns (Lovejoy and Saxton 2012). Communication theorists (McLuhan 1994, Page 1996) long ago noted the power of image over content, linking the liking of the message itself to how well the information in it was retained and kept. Memory and attention-capture studies (Rossiter and Bellman 2005) also reinforce these findings. Pieters and Wedel (2004) found that the image used to convey a message is more important than the content itself as that is what initially captures and holds a viewer's attention.

Political campaigns are no different. However, as noted by Bennett (2012), there can be both positive and negative aspects to using social media in political campaigns for engagement, communications and managing aspects of the campaign. One negative aspect, for example, which is relevant to political marketing and branding is that the very nature of social media itself means that even a large-scale collective-based organisation or movement will find it nearly impossible to stop individuals from personalising the campaign in their own contexts, and therefore possibly diluting the overall momentum or influence of the campaign, an issue noted during the Arab Spring (Bennett and Segerberg 2012).

This was also noted during the 2016 US Presidential race where individuals who formed brand communities through online websites or Facebook sometimes had a negative influence on their favoured candidate by undertaking highly personalised negative attacks through methods such as memes that were then released onto social media.

Due to the interactive nature of imagery on social media, such as memes, the voter consumer has moved from being a passive participant, even at times probably an unwilling one, to being active, engaged and emotionally invested in issues that they find important. This has changed political advertising's strategy range from just awareness or interest building to actually being a tool that can help build relationship, relevance, resonance and response—the four Rs of political advertising strategy in 2017 and beyond.

The ability to alter and personalise political advertising on social media has made imagery have more relevance, and changed how information is disseminated and shared by the voter consumer. Sharing a traditional television advertisement in the past was really only possible through word-of-mouth, the water cooler conversation strategy (Fayard and Weeks 2007). That was a tried and tested tactic of those times. But now an advertisement, be that a video, picture or meme, can be shared within the consumer's target market, adding higher credibility than that offered by the sponsoring brand. That same advertisement can then be liked or emoticoned, commented on, or even shared by others, making the message even more relevant and resonating even stronger than what a television advertisement could ever achieve.

This then has the effect of moving some participants from being passive to being active, not just engaged but having a deeper emotional relationship and investment with the campaign. This remains one of the unexplored areas of political advertising: does the use of visual messaging represent a risk to a campaign and their brands if stakeholders then either start to personalise and run their own communications, especially if this leads to unethical behaviour? Or is the benefit of getting segments, who weren't previously engaged and connected to a campaign, motivated to alter their behaviour to the advantage of the campaign too great to ignore?

YouTube and Political Advertising

YouTube is the second most used search engine in the world, highlighting how consumers see it as a form of information sharing. In more recent times the ability of other social media apps such as Facebook, Twitter, Instagram, Vimeo and even LinkedIn to offer video as well has started to challenge this dominance, but at the same time has led to an explosion in the amount of video content now available on these various platforms. Although any party with a smartphone and a freely available editing package, such as Google Photos or iMovie to name just two, can create a video or even a livecast in a matter of mere minutes, even from YouTube's first formative years political parties differed in the professionalism, strategy and use of this platform.

YouTube has been widely adopted around the world as regardless of the political system it offers the chance to satisfy the four Rs of political advertising with a multitude of stakeholders. It is also free, making it the most cost-effective method of rapidly distributing a political message to a mass market. The fact that it can also be integrated with nearly every other method of digital communication also makes it an ideal platform to raise awareness, although that said not all segments in the market either watch this platform or use the others that help make social media as effective as what it is in 2017.

As noted earlier, and as will be discussed, there is still much debate on how and what makes this medium effective, and if it makes a viewer more passive or active in engagement with a campaign.

YouTube and the Use of Video in the United States

Due to the age, use, access and research on this topic around the world, this section of the chapter will break the analysis into two sections—the United States and the rest of the world. This is not to denigrate the rest of the world but instead merely recognise that the volume of research and practitioner use to date in this area has been done from a US perspective.

The United States has been broken into two time periods, the first being before the impact of mobile devices and applications had really started to be felt in campaigns, the next after that impact had hit and more and more forms of social media began to emerge.

Early Beginnings: 2005–2012

By far the longest, most developed and resourced use of YouTube in the world is in its home market: the United States of America. Research into the use of YouTube in the United States highlights the changing strategy and use of this method in political marketing and campaigns since it was started on 14 February 2005.

Church (2008) was one of the earliest papers to investigate how leaders were using YouTube and how viewers were responding to these messages, although Tan (2007) was the first to note how politicians had already used the platform to launch negative advertisements in the 2006 mid-term elections. Church (2008), using a grounded theory and content analysis approach, found that leaders could better define a narrative on this medium as they could refine their messaging based on the response of the market. Interestingly, he also noted that there were signs that YouTube was a sign of the emergence of the postmodern constituency—or that built around the use of emerging technology and methods in politics, but also one built around the rise of the personal brand (Hughes 2007) or human brand (Eagar et al. 2016). Winograd and Hais (2008) also note the postmodern constituency, but link it more specifically to the then emerging Gen Y and their embrace of the internet and digital technology.

The Obama 2008 campaign changed everything when it came to thinking and directions in political marketing, as has been well noted by authors (Spiller and Bergner 2011). After the 2008 US Presidential elections a whole new amount of research emerged, including many papers that were written for a conference at the University of Massachusetts Amherst in 2009 that specifically considered the use of YouTube at the elections, especially how YouTube had been applied and responded to by voters in the biggest election in the world.

These papers examined everything from attention (Boynton 2009), engagement (Ricke 2010), Congressional-level effects (Williams 2009), integration with Facebook (Robertson et al. 2010) and the role of celebrity in leadership (Savoie 2009).

They laid the groundwork for researchers and practitioners into how to start using the platform for more than just reposting content, from creating celebrities out of leader brands, to posting continuous content as a form of engagement and relationship building, and early steps into segmentation of value offerings at more micro levels than what television allowed.

Of all the papers that did emerge from the 2008 campaign, the one of note was the more strategic approach in using YouTube in a campaign as discussed by Ridout et al. (2010). This paper not only examined over 3500 YouTube videos but also considered what had worked and what hadn't from a format and structure perspective. What Ridout et al. (2010) found was that although there was no pattern to what made one advertisement more viewed than another from a source and format perspective, the 30-second video was more likely to be used in news stories because of its length. Klotz (2010) noted similar findings, that candidates and parties had not adapted that much to the new-found flexibility of the platform, either reposting television advertisements they had made or restricting content to a few minutes or less mainly because they still hadn't developed methods and strategy on how to use the platform as part of a wider narrative or communications campaign.

The hallmark of this first initial period of YouTube was one of learning by campaigns and practitioners of what this platform could allow, and how postmodern constituency had changed the political consumer from being an information receiver to being a co-creator of information, more engaged and connected with campaigns, especially those that had a celebrity as a leader, such as the Obama campaign of 2008.

Towards the end of this period as the information age took hold and more, and more competitors to YouTube emerged on various platforms, technology once again helped transform the use of YouTube within campaigns.

Current Time Frame: 2013–2017+

As more and more media applications emerged and transformed themselves from just a single application to multiple applications, for example, Instagram allowing messaging and videos, Twitter allowing livestreaming, images and video, and Facebook allowing basically anything, the use of YouTube also changed.

In a strategy sense some interesting characteristics from social media in general started to be seen in political advertising. The first of these was the term "slacktivist" or basically someone who may be engaged and have a relationship with a campaign through social media, even creating content, but then failed to turn this into behaviour through either voting or adopting or changing their behaviour in line with what the campaign was asking. Slacktivists are seen as one of the negatives of YouTube, and social media in general, making engagement not an accurate predictor of either likely behaviour or commitment to a cause or campaign (Glenn 2015). Some (Christensen 2011, Rotman et al. 2011) have attributed slacktivisim to being more likely to happen to Gen Y and the millennials. Whatever the reason, it does show that at the end of the day for some YouTube is just an awareness and engagement tool, it still does not have enough power to switch interest to behavioural change.

User-generated content has been another hallmark of this period. As mobile devices and apps started to filter through the population, content production became as simple as a few taps on a screen. Overall, YouTube itself has discussed this trend as it notes that every second 400 hours of content is uploaded to its site (Statista 2016). With the quality of the devices improving so too did production quality, and anyone could post high-quality material to YouTube in seconds.

This has helped change the speed and nature of campaigning, with user-made content sometimes having higher effectiveness as the credibility of the source can be more trusted than a political brand and be uploaded quicker than anything from a major brand. This creates the perception that the user content is more engaged with an issue than the politician or creating a sense that the user content comes from a grassroots perspective and therefore is more of a "voice of the people" style video than what could be possible from a more commercialised political brand.

User-generated content can also help a new political brand quickly establish itself and engage with its market, giving it a more innovative, dynamic and connected feel. User content can help lower the perceived risk or cost of supporting a new brand, but also help reinforce brand associations and imagery, all at the same time as minimising a drain on resources. The transferability of content such as this means that a brand can also utilise this type of content quickly across multiple social media and communication sources, further maximising the impact from the content and improving the reach of the communications and the market appeal of the brand.

However, the uncontrolled nature of user-generated content can also harm a brand. YouTube videos only take as long to upload as an internet connection allows, and content can remain undiscovered by a brand for hours, or even days, until noticed. Even here, unless such content breaches YouTube's content guidelines, it is likely to stay online, even if that content may not be what the brand wants to see. Whilst this harm can be somewhat minimised by brands making direct appeals to the user to either modify or remove the content, this will only be effective if the user responds to this appeal.

In the age of social media, it is just not larger, more commercial stakeholders, such as the Super PAC's in the United States, that may run campaigns that may benefit or harm other political brands but also a user with a large following on a social media platform that may have only a relationship with a brand in the most flimsy of electronic ways.

Fake and Bot Accounts

One of the bigger disadvantages of YouTube as a political advertising tool is the prevalence of fake and bot accounts. These accounts can not only post content but also comments, diluting the effectiveness of a video by turning the comments on a video into either a link to a counter-video or an advertisement for who knows what, and discouraging other users from providing feedback and engaging with the content.

YouTube is a good form of qualitative market research. It provides quick in-depth feedback from viewers, and the statistics allow a user to see how quickly a video is diffused through a market, who is watching (age, gender, location), for how long, from where, using what platform or device (desktop or mobile), and if they liked or disliked the video. However, all of these stats can be diluted or made ineffectual by the behaviour of bot or fake accounts.

Bot and fake accounts can also post content, which in recent times around the world has come in handy for those seeking to leak material that may be damaging or harmful but may come from within a brand. Content posted by a bot or a fake account may also have far more sinister motives and be used to try and influence the outcome of an election. As YouTube is free and an account can be set up fairly easily, a fake or bot account used for more strategic or harmful purposes can flood the platform with content and even be used to target certain segments with material, allegations that were raised about certain accounts during the 2016 US Presidential election, but ones that have also been noted in elections around the world as well where YouTube can be accessed.

Whilst the platform has the existence and darker strategic uses of these sorts of accounts, and is implementing controls to limit the harm, the cause or influence they have, it is unknown if in the short period of time that these accounts are active they may in fact be having an impact on election outcomes.

Trolling

Trolling on social media platforms is becoming of more concern to society, users and many political organisations due to the harmful impacts it has in multiple contexts. YouTube is no different.

Trolling has been linked to fake and bot accounts, but it can also be carried out by actors that may support a political brand but also may not have a formal relationship with one. These brand partisans or fanatics see acting on behalf of a brand as part of their loyalty and commitment to that brand. With very few brands taking a stand on this sort of behaviour by supporters, it is also starting to become more entrenched in political systems around the world.

Trolls on YouTube have the same aims as trolls on other media platforms. These can be summarised as follows:

- Disengagement with the political process
- Distrust of political actors
- Discredit political actors on key attributes and characteristics.
- Attack other brand supporters and loyalists.
- Distract from other political brand narratives.
- Create awareness of their supported brand or issue.

YouTube Outside the United States

Chen (2008) did one of the very first studies into how YouTube was used by a political party outside the United States and found that early Australian political parties differed in how they saw the platform as a communications method. Although in recent times this has most definitely altered in a methods context, the professionalism of the content, and the quantity, is still very much dependent on the resources a party has available to it. Chen (2008) also noted that even in these early years the level of engagement and interaction with this media was far higher than more traditional forms, although perhaps this could also be due to the novelty and innovativeness of the media at the time.

There have also been studies done in other nations, looking into the effect of YouTube from a cross-cultural perspective. One thing that does seem to be an interesting finding in studies done outside the United States is that political system does not have a significant influence on the impact of YouTube. This could indicate that perhaps the way political information is processed by voters around the world is more similar than what has been previously assumed. The one common factor regardless of system is the lack of credibility and faith many have in politicians, regardless of country, system or culture.

These findings support the notion that the impact communications is having on political systems and voters is not just restricted to certain democractic systems, but is also having a broader societal impact. As the next generation embrace social and digital media earlier than other generations before them this also means that this impact is having a far earlier influence in our lives on our attitudes and perceptions towards political brands than what was previously assumed.

STRATEGIES OF VIDEO ON SOCIAL MEDIA

The use of video on social media is becoming more and more widespread. Statistics reveal that the younger the generation is, the more likely that their preferred media platform is to be one of the newer formats, such as social media, the internet or even those accessible through casting devices such as Google's Chromecast and Apple TV. Even though these platforms also carry the more traditional news or news magazine current affairs style television programmes, younger markets are preferring to have their news and current affairs information served to them in a simpler, more digestable format from one of the more modern and innovative news networks such as Vice News, BuzzFeed or a similar channel.

It is this change in how a voter receives, engages with and understands information that has had the most profound effect on political advertising in the last decade. Although some may attribute some of the changes in use and effectiveness of political advertising to systems or voluntary or non-voluntary voting, there is more support for the notion that how information is processed, gathered and received by a consumer has had the greater impact.

Theorists such as Richard Thaler and the theory of nudge, and Annie Lang's seminal lifetime work in information processing, including that in political communication and advertising, across the last three decades, also demonstrates the changing nature and effectiveness of information in 2017.

What is being witnessed now is that change moving from being less significant to highly significant as the population ages and technological innovations and tools are diffused in the population and become more widespread in use. Election nights spent around a television to await the reading of results have been replaced by social media feeds and near real-time updating by electoral authorities of results on websites and applications. The demand upon electoral systems for this information has never been greater. This lack of patience for electoral results by some in younger demographics has led to increased calls for more electronic forms of voting, such as through apps and websites, to speed up the results process and allow for a faster democratic process.

Information change and variation in the age of new media has also helped move political advertising from a reliance upon the television commercial being the workhorse of the communication of the value offering to having a multifaceted use from livecasting to maintaining and even rewarding those with a relationship with the political brand. For those observers, practitioners and researchers of political advertising it is far more important to understand the change of information sought by those who vote than what techniques may be used to carry a message. After all it is how a voter uses information that is more likely to influence their behaviour than how they may be influenced by one form of communication.

Livecasting

Livecasting has been a significant change in the use of political advertising. YouTube, Facebook, Twitter and many other platforms allow for the livecasting of content, usually for only minimal cost. This has turned content producers from just supplying on-demand content such as videos to being also content broadcasters, able to rival traditional media channels and have greater control on the messaging broadcast.

It has also helped with relationship building and brand loyalty by offering those who are members of the organisation or who may subscribe to the channel a chance to being given either notification of these events or the chance to participate through asking questions. They also provide a valuable source of quick marketing research to political brands on platforms such as Facebook through viewer responses using emoticons, comments and shares. However, the use of this, and how effective this is for a political brand, is still the subject of debate.

However, live casting is one method that has changed political advertising from just being one directional to being more like a constant conversation that a political brand has with a market.

CUSTOMER LOYALTY, ENGAGEMENT AND REAL-TIME RESEARCH

Apart from live casts, the use of video on social media platforms allows for far more micro-targeting and engagement than what was otherwise possible. Whilst many marketers in the commercial world work towards a co-created or personalised value experience and offering, politics is not quite at that level—yet. However, with some of these communication methods being used, in combination with the use of big data and customer insights that every year eclipse that of the year before, there may yet be a day when a form of political advertising may become customised for the viewer or person who observes it.

For now, though, political brands can still use digital forms of dynamic political advertising to enhance customer loyalty, deepen engagement and conduct and analyse real-time research.

NEGATIVES OF ONLINE VIDEO AND DYNAMIC FORMS OF POLITICAL ADVERTISING

Trolling

As already discussed, trolling is one of the most negative side effects from using online videos in political advertising.

Fake and Bot Accounts

Whilst previous discussion in this chapter has examined fake and bot accounts, it will be up to electoral authorities and even political parties themselves to undertake more ethical practices in this area to prevent this method from harming the use of the digital space for political advertising.

ENGAGEMENT, LIKING AND TRUST OF POLITICAL BRANDS AND INSTITUTIONS

Video has not always been seen as increasing engagement and liking of political brands and institutions (Lau et al. 2007, Brader 2005). In fact a quick glance at the YouTube, Facebook and Twitter accounts of most large political brands and their content highlights how few comments are positive or from genuinely engaged voters whom the campaign is targeting. That is not to say, though, that they aren't watching, but perhaps they are wise enough not to comment and face the wrath of the trolls who may read their opinions.

But with pre-existing attitudes and opinions towards political brands being at record lows, more content and engagement may not be what many want unless it is in a form that is going to be motivationally relevant. This area does need further research to explore how online political advertising is affecting the emotional responses towards political brands but there is no doubt that according to some there are concerns in this area.

OTHER ACTORS IN POLITICAL EXCHANGES ACTING UNETHICALLY

The ability to run a professional campaign in politics has never been just restricted to political brands, with there being several notable campaigns around the world of other successful political advertising campaigns from the environment to mining. However social, digital and mobile marketing has allowed some actors behind these campaigns to do so with a higher degree of anonymity than in the past. With anonymity comes confidence to act and behave in ways that are ethically questionable at best, illegal and exploitative at worst.

Whilst there have been examples all around the world in the last decade of the use of digital methods to influence campaigns, nowhere else was the use and ownership of political advertising on online platforms more obscured and used at such a large scale than in the United States in 2016.

In 2017 it was revealed by Facebook that a substantial number of political advertisements were purchased by a likely foreign actor, although who exactly that actor was and who might be funding them is probably going to remain a secret worthy of the *X-Files*. YouTube has also revealed that it is likely that foreign actors also purchased advertisements for use in the 2016 US elections.

Again, the identity of these actors may never be truly known. But it does raise the issue that this could happen to any campaign in any place in the world that uses these platforms. After all, these are private organisations who are not required to have the same standards as larger broadcasters in traditional media. In fairness though these new media outlets process millions of items of visual content every month and can't be expected to have the resources or ability to screen every single one of them.

This does lead to the issue that governments need to rapidly change existing electoral laws to bring them up to what is actually happening in campaigns, not an ideal legalistic Utopia based on everyone behaving themselves. That is one thing that will never happen when it comes to political marketing in any part of the world.

Access to Technology and Resource Management

User-generated content may help brands but eventually they will need to start to improve the production standards to match that of the bigger brands or start to lose viewers to other options, be they political or otherwise. Therefore, in a way the use of technology may have also deepened the digital divide in politics. Finding people with the resources and skills to match the commercial operators that now operate for the major brands is difficult for minor brands.

One of the new arms races in political advertising isn't just about who can purchase the most airtime on television, but who can make the slickest communications. Another example in this area is the use of infographics, which can be difficult and time consuming to put together unless you have the knowhow and the right information, but is becoming important as an information medium for consumers.

It can only be hoped that campaign and election reforms in the area of communications also consider a cap on the resources used by all parties if the term free, fair and frequent elections is to have any significant meaning in the digital age.

Simplification of Policy Formulation, Information and Lack of Debate

As noted by Schupp et al. (2000), for someone to want to pay attention to your message for a prolonged period of time it needs to be motivationally relevant. That can only occur in the first place if the attitude towards the brand and the message itself is positive, along with of course being relevant to the viewer.

To try and overcome these issues with dynamic content political brands have resorted to similar strategies used by some commercial brands to engage consumers for more than the opening few seconds of an advertisement or message. One of these has been to minimise content in advertisements and messages, just focusing on more the "headline" or key pieces of information. Whilst this is understandable with the above theory in mind, one of the unintended consequences has been that for many viewers details on policy have become sparse and hard to find.

For the great majority of viewers on the vast majority of issues this is of no real great concern as they have a negative attitude towards any political message and probably nearly all political brands. However, for many political analysts, scientists and researchers, and for many involved with a specific issue, that has meant a lack of detail and depth on policy. Policy has become market driven and with only sufficient information to sway or alter behaviour.

Some recent examples of where some have highlighted this simplification of information have been with Brexit in 2016 and the US elections in 2016 at nearly all levels, similarly in Australia the successful "Mediscare" campaign utilised people's lack of information and knowledge of the governance of the scheme to create the perception that the government intended to privatise the scheme when it had never stated any intention to do so.

Whilst there are more factors that have contributed to this than just video, it has been a reason why policy discussion has moved from detail to the concise.

The Relationship Between Experiential, Brand Personality and Relationship: What Makes Video on Social Media Different to Television Advertising

Video is just one form of political advertising. And political advertising is the primary strategic tool to convey a value offering in many markets, but not all, such as in Japan where it is rarely used and grassroots methods are still the main method.

However, as part of an integrated campaign, and designed to be positive, it can be used to make a political brand more experiential (Shobeiri et al. 2013) and have more of a personality (Aaker 1997) than what may be the case if using only traditional media. A single message on an online platform can also have more impact than a single television advertisement since the context it can be viewed on may be as equally as dynamic as the message itself. For example, a person using social media on a long commute may actually pay more attention to a political advertisement as they may not be as distracted as they may be at home where they may have more screens open along with other noise.

Social media allows for a more demand-driven perspective from a viewer—a consumer usually needs to seek out that message to view it. This can make the message more of an experience, have a stronger resonance and relevance to it than a television advertisement, and associate a certain personality with a brand. There does need to be more research to support this analysis but there is emerging evidence of how voters are using social media to suggest that this is the case.

The experience social media allows is also far different from traditional forms of political advertising. Media can be instantly shared, liked or commented upon, and emoticons add another element of experience and engagement that traditional media doesn't allow. In seconds an ad can reach every corner of the market, with shared content between users having a higher source credibility than what would be possible from an advertisement from a political brand or other actor. A user can even create their own content as a response, from using a gif, image, meme or even a video, uploading that in the comments section of a page in near real time. The UKIP "Breaking Point" ad was an example of an ad that was shared, liked, commented on and responded to within hours of its release.

It is this higher level of experience and engagement on social media platforms that is slowly seeing the decreased use of traditional forms of political advertising. As discussed in earlier chapters, television advertising is slowly losing its effectiveness. This effect is more pronounced and dramatic where the advertising is negative as people find advertisements about value loss less relevant and engaging than positive messages about value gain. There needs to be a re-examination of televised political advertising, using more modern methods such as psychophysiological responses and more reflective studies where participants watch a television show with advertising breaks inserted as they would at home, and not singular political advertisements that could skew the results.

Of note here is how most research into televised political advertising has been done before as a contrast to how that research is conducted in 2017. This is not to fault or be critical of all prior research, more to say that social media allows for the capturing of how consumers responded in the context and environment, and in real time, to political messages they saw.

Over time as social media becomes used as the primary communication tool by more and more of the population, the markets' engagement and experience with political advertising will become more personal and more direct. This change will create a better experience for the political consumer, but only if political brands are willing enough to use more positive advertising and less negative advertising.

CONCLUSION

Social media is the most transformative tool that has happened to political advertising since colour television became the norm. It has changed the engagement, experience and emotional responses of consumers for consumers, and allowed instantaneous measurement of the effectiveness of messages. Consumers can also use social media to become content creators, co-creating value with brands, other consumers and other actors to even further heighten emotional responses and experiences with political brands.

These aspects of social media are changing the use and effectiveness of advertising done on traditional media, such as television, but at the same time this change may yet prolong the life of some of these forms as they can then be used to communicate to multiple segments different value offerings in the one single message to a mass market that social media just can't do right now.

Whilst there is justifiable buzz and hype around social media, this should be kept in check by the fact that right now television is still the boss in many markets, but it is doing itself and its users no favours through the reckless pursuit of negative messages that are only driving further gaps between brand, consumer and experience.

REFERENCES

Aaker, J. L. (1997). Dimensions of brand personality. *Journal of Marketing Research, 34*(3), 347–356.

Bennett, W. L. (2012). The personalization of politics: Political identity, social media, and changing patterns of participation. *The ANNALS of the American Academy of Political and Social Science, 644*(1), 20–39.

Bennett, W. L., & Segerberg, A. (2012). The logic of connective action: Digital media and the personalization of contentious politics. *Information, Communication & Society, 15*(5), 739–768.

Boynton, G. R. (2009). *What if you had a choice?* Paper presented at the 2009 Annual Meeting of the American Political Science Association, Toronto, ON, Canada.

Brader, T. (2005). Striking a responsive chord: How political ads motivate and persuade voters by appealing to emotions. *American Journal of Political Science, 49*(2), 388–405.

Bu, J., Tan, S., Chen, C., Wang, C., Wu, H., Zhang, L., & He, X. (2010, October). Music recommendation by unified hypergraph: Combining social media information and music content. In *Proceedings of the 18th ACM international conference on Multimedia* (pp. 391–400). ACM.

Chen, P. J. (2008). Australian political parties' use of YouTube 2007. *Communication, Politics & Culture, 41*(1), 114.

Christensen, H. S. (2011). Political activities on the Internet: Slacktivism or political participation by other means? *First Monday, 16*(2).

Church, S. (2008). *A content analyses of presidential candidates' video clips on YouTube.* Doctoral dissertation, Master thesis, Department of Communication of Southern Utah University.

Eagar, T., Dann, S., & Dann, S. (2016). Classifying the narrated# selfie: Genre typing human-branding activity. *European Journal of Marketing, 50*(9/10), 1835–1857.

Fayard, A. L., & Weeks, J. (2007). Photocopiers and water-coolers: The affordances of informal interaction. *Organization Studies, 28*(5), 605–634.

Glenn, C. L. (2015). Activism or "slacktivism?": Digital media and organizing for social change. *Communication Teacher, 29*(2), 81–85.

Hughes, A. (2007). Personal brands: An exploratory analysis of personal brands in Australian political marketing. In *Australia and New Zealand Marketing Academy Conference*, 3–5 December 2007, University of Otago, Dunedin.

Klotz, R. J. (2010). The sidetracked 2008 YouTube senate campaign. *Journal of Information Technology & Politics, 7*(2–3), 110–123.

Lau, R. R., Sigelman, L., & Rovner, I. B. (2007). The effects of negative political campaigns: A meta analytic reassessment. *Journal of Politics, 69*(4), 1176–1209.

Lovejoy, K., & Saxton, G. D. (2012). Information, community, and action: How nonprofit organizations use social media. *Journal of Computer-Mediated Communication, 17*(3), 337–353.

McLuhan, M. (1994). *Understanding media: The extensions of man.* MIT Press.

Page, B. I. (1996). The mass media as political actors. *PS: Political Science and Politics, 29*(1), 20–24.

Pieters, R., & Wedel, M. (2004). Attention capture and transfer in advertising: Brand, pictorial, and text-size effects. *Journal of Marketing, 68*(2), 36–50.

Ricke, L. (2010). A new opportunity for democratic engagement: The CNN-YouTube presidential candidate debates. *Journal of Information Technology & Politics, 7*(2–3), 202–215.

Ridout, T. N., Franklin Fowler, E., & Branstetter, J. (2010). *Political advertising in the 21st century: The rise of the YouTube ad.* Paper prepared for the American Political Science Association Conference.

Robertson, S. P., Vatrapu, R. K., & Medina, R. (2010). Online video "friends" social networking: Overlapping online public spheres in the 2008 U.S. Presidential election. *Journal of Information Technology & Politics, 7,* 182–201.

Rossiter, J. R., & Bellman, S. (2005). *Marketing communications: Theory and applications.* London: Prentice-Hall.

Rotman, D., Vieweg, S., Yardi, S., Chi, E., Preece, J., Shneiderman, B., ... Glaisyer, T. (2011, May). From slacktivism to activism: Participatory culture in the age of social media. In *CHI'11 Extended Abstracts on Human Factors in Computing Systems* (pp. 819–822). ACM.

Sashi, C. M. (2012). Customer engagement, buyer-seller relationships, and social media. *Management Decision, 50*(2), 253–272.

Savoie, H. (2009). John McCain gets BarackRoll'd: Authorship, culture, and community on YouTube. *ScholarWorks@ UMass Amherst*, 177.

Schupp, H. T., Cuthbert, B. N., Bradley, M. M., Cacioppo, J. T., Ito, T., & Lang, P. J. (2000). Affective picture processing: The late positive potential is modulated by motivational relevance. *Psychophysiology, 37*(2), 257–261.

Shobeiri, S., Laroche, M., & Mazaheri, E. (2013). Shaping e-retailer's website personality: The importance of experiential marketing. *Journal of Retailing and Consumer Services, 20*(1), 102–110.

Spiller, L. D., & Bergner, J. (2011). *Branding the candidate: Marketing strategies to win your vote*. ABC-CLIO.

Statista. (2016). YouTube statistics and facts. Retrieved December 20, 2017, from https://www.statista.com/topics/2019/youtube/

Tan, E. (2007). Look out, '08 candidates: YouTube users are watching. *Advertising Age, 78*(19), 4.

Williams, C. B. (2009). What is a social network worth? Facebook and Vote Share in the 2008 presidential primaries. In *Annual Meeting of the American Political Science Association*.

Winograd, M., & Hais, M. D. (2008). *Millennial makeover: MySpace, YouTube, and the future of American politics*. Rutgers University Press.

Xiang, Z., & Gretzel, U. (2010). Role of social media in online travel information search. *Tourism Management, 31*(2), 179–188.

CHAPTER 5

Social and Digital Media: Creating, Engaging and Motivating Relationships

Abstract Political advertising on social, mobile and digital media used with a market driven perspective has changed how voters engage, experience and embrace political brands and candidates. This chapter explores how the shift from a unidirectional approach of stakeholder to voter has now become a two-way conversation that can occur across multiple platforms in the space of seconds rather than days or weeks as was the case in the past.

This change has benefitted all parties regardless of size or system as they can now move a voter from passive to active and active to volunteer or co-producer of content and ideas. A minor party is able to use these methods to become more entrepreneurial in behaviour, even acting as a disruptor in more established systems such as seen in the Obama campaign of 2008 or even through the Pirate Party in Iceland.

Keywords Social media • NationBuilder • Google • Marketing campaign • Market research

© The Author(s) 2018
A. Hughes, *Market Driven Political Advertising*,
Palgrave Studies in Political Marketing and Management,
https://doi.org/10.1007/978-3-319-77730-6_5

INTRODUCTION

This chapter will look at how political advertising is moving from just one-directional mass communication as was the case with traditional media to being about two-way communication and relationship building. It is also enabling political organisations and candidates to obtain real-time data and feedback on policies and thus allow a much more market-driven approach.

Political advertising on social media is also being used not just for awareness raising but also to connect with and engage with volunteers who may not be party members. This is then connected with another app, such as NationBuilder, to allow for rapid and direct involvement of volunteers into a campaign.

The data created by using political advertising on social media and the internet is also being used and correlated with existing databases to drive deeper insights into voting and consumer behaviour in the political marketplace, a trend which is assisting minor parties to compete with the larger brands.

The chapter will end with a word of caution on the use of social media as a predictor of election outcomes. This will be that a person's level of engagement on social media is not an accurate predictor of actual election outcomes, as seen by election results such as Brexit and the 2016 US Presidential elections.

SOCIAL MEDIA—POLITICAL e-MANAGEMENT

NationBuilder

Social media has provided political parties with just not the ability to engage and communicate with target markets and voters but also to manage volunteers, party members and the campaign itself.

For example, NationBuilder, an early leader in party management and organisation, has been used by many political organisations as a way to organise volunteers and keep track of campaign methods such as door knocking.

The scalability of this software programme has made it the go-to programme of choice for campaigns ranging from local council elections to the largest campaigns in recent times such as Trump's 2016 campaign and Brexit (Jones 2016). As it can incorporate other programmes such as MailChimp, Wordpress and even Paypal to help provide a fundraising and donation platform, it's adaptability makes it a useful tool in any campaign.

Where it can really assist a campaign though is access to databases, for a cost of course.

This means for a political brand seeking to establish itself very quickly but also wanting to take advantage of weaknesses in existing markets and party positions. NationBuilder is the sort of tool that makes party and campaign management one less distraction from running an effective campaign. The use of data in this way can turn a small or minor party from being seen as an irrelevance to having an image of a cool disruptor, like the Pirate Party in Iceland, or even the Greens in many nations.

The integration of big data like this is not just unique to NationBuilder but perhaps they, along with the bigger political analytic firms of Cambridge Analytica and Crosby Textor, highlight just how much development there has been in political management alongside political marketing with the use and adoption of technology.

But for the right amount of money, and with the right sort of thinking, a political brand can very quickly establish itself in a market, engage with micro-segments on issue-based platforms, create customised low-risk value offerings and exchanges, but at the same time manage volunteers, donations, communications, databases and campaigns through a few clicks of a mouse. This makes it sound as if any party anywhere is able to do this but it has to be remembered that this works best in a democracy where a party can utilise the free market that may exist.

And, of course, even if a party not in a democracy were to use an app such as this, the party culture would have to be willing to not only use this form of management but also have a value and belief system in place where they would to use it across the entire organisation and have faith in its design and methods. This is not for every party.

However, use of these apps is not just restricted to purely political actors. Actors in political markets, such as non-profits and non-government organisations, have also become keen users of these sorts of organiser apps, especially NationBuilder (Jones 2016), which ensures that at times there is a clear permeation in the relationship between those who work in the nonprofit sector and those that work in the political one.

NationBuilder may be one of the more publicly, better known and sophisticated applications out there but it is by no means shadowy unlike perhaps some of the existing databases and software programmes used by major parties around the world. They also source information from social media or anywhere else that doesn't breach electoral guidelines that have turned consumers' data into valuable pieces of information that have provided insights that campaign managers of old could only dream about or afford if they worked for a large organisation.

Is it effective? It most definitely is according to those who have spoken publicly about it to date (Jones 2016; Heath 2017). Even for small brands the cost of the most basic packages ($29 up to the $160 a month premium bundle) on NationBuilder is affordable and can have a transformative effect on political management. There could even be an argument made that NationBuilder is making democracy and politics more effective, and more market focused and driven.

The age of populist politics may be here but perhaps the better term when it comes to integrating tools such as NationBuilder is democratic revival and creating a sense of real change with people-led movements that haven't existed for a while. Even using a Kantian perspective it could be argued that these sorts of applications are assisting in a redistribution of power and knowledge, helping minor and independent brands achieve better electoral success and representation.

Is it ethical? NationBuilder, in the places it is used, is not breaking any laws nor should it be seen as being unethical as it is merely a tool or method for a modern political organisation or movement. It is not an agenda setter or agent of change for an organisation, movement or leader. Such issues are still up to those who manage the campaign and the organisation. However, the use of technology does raise the issue of the need for campaign caps on expenditure to be more reflective of political organisation behaviour in the digital age and include these types of methods, tools and activities.

Although the use of databases in apps such as NationBuilder is a different story altogether in the digital age. The ethics of database use has been well explored (Cannon 2002, Milne 2000) and noted as an area of future concern for researchers and practitioners (Schlegelmilch and Öberseder 2010). From an evidence-based perspective data breaches of the scale that Cambridge Analytica suffered (Lapowsky 2017), and the rise of hackers (just ask the Hillary Clinton campaign), either state sponsored or not, may mean that the use of databases should also come along with the use of cutting-edge security and even protections from governments.

Other Tools for e-Management

As mentioned, NationBuilder is not the only app that can be used for political and campaign management. *Off-the-shelf software programmes* like Microsoft Office (think Excel, Outlook and Access) and free tools through *cloud-based platforms* such as Google Docs, Sheets and Slides can offer a political organisation data and management tools the likes of which were not available even five years ago.

The use of free cloud-based software programmes, such as Google, has in particular allowed a campaign to be active regardless of the time, day or even campaign team and create a sense of momentum, enthusiasm, dynamism and innovation amongst target markets than what could be possible relying upon older methods. Not to mention, Google allows for integration of search, websites and YouTube functions and tracking of advertising effectiveness through the use of Adwords that can help push a political brand closer to the coveted top three spots in a Google search undertaken by a consumer.

There are even apps for uploading documents and files onto websites, such as Storify, that help a consumer find information more naturally without feeling as though they are being pushed in a certain direction. Gone are the days of UK Labour handing out their policy "manifesto" on a red USB or even the data dumps of zip files that made Wikileaks infamous.

A party or movement can easily *manage images* on platforms such as Flickr, Imgur, Tumblr and even Pinterest, providing a way to control the use of static images but also providing important data on how these images are being viewed, downloaded and used by people. Established social media sites also allow for this but these are sites that specifically can be used for images.

Marketing campaign software, such as Slack, can be readily adapted to a political movement or campaign. Slack is an app that allows for anyone with a mobile device to manage and connect with other people using social media login details in a safe, secure and intimate way. Slack may have less functionality compared to NationBuilder but it is also far quicker to set up, connect other users and start to manage a campaign and communications.

Market research has been simplified and opened up to anyone through the use of brands such as SurveyMonkey, SurveyGizmo or Google forms although SurveyMonkey is the preferred brand here because it allows for integration with MailChimp. Other survey software such as Qualtrics offer more functionality and levels of analysis but come with a higher price tag and may often be out of the reach of many in politics.

Social media management can be done through applications such as TweetDeck, HootSuite, Insightly or SproutSocial, amongst a cavalcade of others that can schedule and manage posts, and used to manage followers on the various social media platforms. Again many platforms have these features built in but they don't allow for integration across a wide range of devices and platforms.

Blogs and *websites* offer another platform in which to engage, manage and connect with different stakeholders. Many websites of political organisations and movements now have login and dashboard features where those with access can not only get direct information about activities but also engage and converse with others involved in the campaign. They also provide a way to buy and distribute campaign merchandise, as was seen most noticeably in the Hillary campaign of 2016, and get member-only materials.

They have also allowed many who are interested in a campaign or movement the chance to have a low-risk and low-involvement opportunity to become active or join a campaign. Australia's GetUp! and change.org in the United States are issue-based movement organisations that do exactly that, although change.org is more of a social and political entrepreneurship platform that allows anyone to start a petition on nearly any issue.

A blog and website can also offer more secure ways of relationship building through online community brand forums. Whilst closed groups on social media can also allow this level of functionality and engagement, more specifically set up forums and discussion boards, even though a relatively old technology, still allow for a more safe, secure and open way for the more committed to engage in policy discussions.

Crowd funding websites such as kickstarter, indiegogo and gofundme amongst others have given organisations, movements and individuals the chance to raise funds and awareness simultaneously and to challenge the existing frameworks used by larger parties and movements. It should be noted here that there are three main types of crowdfunding websites based on what the organisation is exchanging for value: rewards, equity or donations. Most political organisations that use crowdfunding do so as part of a broader donations or even rewards-based system, as in a donation or purchase may obtain or unlock a certain reward. There are also some websites, such as GlobalGiving, that are specifically aimed at raising money for project-based activities by a nonprofit or cause, although there have been very few examples of political organisations using this platform.

Crowdsourcing can also help political organisations with running campaigns through designing campaign communications, materials and merchandise. Websites such as 99designs or CafePress allow for a campaign to obtain at a low-cost campaign advertising materials and merchandise that can rival that of the larger parties. Crowdsourcing can also of course help with even the more grassroots level of political advertising activities, such as getting volunteers for door knocking, leaflet drops, personnel for stands, resources for campaign promotions and communications, or even guest speakers for events.

Whilst there may be some who see the digital age when it comes to political advertising and communications as being one of fear and loss of privacy, there is no doubt that it has also opened up a whole range of possibilities and opportunities for parties, especially minor parties and candidates, around the world that would not have been possible if political advertising had been anchored to the more traditional methods and activities that undoubtedly favoured the major parties.

INTEGRATION OF BIG DATA FROM SOCIAL MEDIA WITH CAMPAIGN DATA—NEW FRONTIERS

As discussed above big data is the new frontier for campaigns, offering unparalleled insights into voters that have never been available before. As more and more of our lives moves into a cloud-based database somewhere run by someone, or perhaps even a bot, this information is becoming more and more accessible. It was once said (Solomon et al. 2013) that the hardest information to obtain on someone was psychographic (our personality, attitudes and opinions) and behavioural (how we behave and respond to different stimuli and times) as these remained the most closely guarded domains of an individual.

Social media changed all of that within a decade. In the information era the huge amount of data that is produced every day about our lives from everything from social media accounts, to loyalty schemes run by large retailers, has placed the value of our information at times in the billions of dollars (Schmitt et al. 2013). We are now the consumer and the product. This information when combined can enable those with the access, knowledge and resources to nearly build a complete picture of someone and how they might behave in certain situations.

This use of big data and predictive analytics has already seen the integration of the results of this information by governments and other organisations with practical implementations of nudge theory, or behavioural economics as made famous by Richard Thaler who won the 2017 Nobel Prize for Economics for his work in this area. Nudge theory is defined by Thaler and Sunstein (2008) as being:

A nudge, as we will use the term, is any aspect of the choice architecture that alters people's behavior in a predictable way without forbidding any options or significantly changing their economic incentives. To count as a mere nudge, the intervention must be easy and cheap to avoid. Nudges are not mandates. Putting fruit at eye level counts as a nudge. Banning junk food does not.

Nudge theory's awareness with social and political marketers was helped when then Prime Minister of the United Kingdom, David Cameron, and then US President Barrack Obama, stated that they had read the book and had asked some government departments to investigate how they could use nudge in more of their programmes and campaigns. This area of marketing is growing more and more in use around the world as society becomes more interested and aware of the damage of some types of behaviours, which sometimes are caused by marketers of commercial products.

In a political campaign this knowledge is not the sort of thing Kant would see as empowering or altering power elites in the world. If anything it gives those with the resources and knowledge the opportunity to further entrench their positions or to stop disruptors or challengers from becoming long-term rivals. As Sir Francis Bacon once said, knowledge is power and those with the knowledge of how to use a database are becoming very powerful people in modern campaigning.

A firm such as Cambridge Analytica can use the knowledge and information from multiple database integrations to nearly accurately predict how someone may rank different issues, how they may respond to different policies on those issues and then what sort of message on what sort of platform would be the most effective to display to that person. Digital platforms such as Twitter allow for advertisements to be nearly personalised based on the use of the information from databases, similar to what happened in the United States in 2016 when Cambridge Analytica was able to have 50,000 variations on one message that appeared on Facebook and Twitter (Cadwalladr 2016; Lapowsky 2016).

Cambridge Analytica are not the only firm and they were not the first firm to use big data in politics, but they were the first to do it on a large national scale through firstly the United Kingdom and then the United States. They were also the first to incorporate the ability to target specific issues, realising that party identification built around a broad-based values platform had long ago disappeared from many voters and instead been replaced by a more individual driven view of exchange and offering, a WIIFY philosophy—What's In It For You (or Me).

If the use of big data is combined with a method such as nudge then this becomes a very potent tool that few can match. It can mobilise and engage those who perhaps would have been overlooked using more traditional campaign analytics. The Trump campaign used big data to target those who had identified as an issue being white, middle-aged male, working class and as being neglected by existing power elites to nudge their behaviour towards voting Republican, channelling anger into action at the ballot box in such unprecedented numbers that no modelling from the Democrats could identify this swing taking place.

Other campaigns around the world have also used big data in this way: in France Emmanuel Macron energised and connected with voters who wanted change on specific issues more than brand loyalty to sweep two election wins: the Presidential ones and then that of the Parliament. Justin Trudeau in Canada also did the same, again using issue-based campaigning to create momentum and to create the perception that he would change the power dynamics if elected to allow for a more engaged and dynamic government. Even in 2017 in Kenya there have been allegations that Cambridge Analytica is active and using its techniques and methods there.

For the fans of purely marketing-based democracy and political systems, populist politics as it were, then perhaps this is no bad thing as the market is getting what it wants. Yet around the world when some of these outcomes have occurred, such as with Brexit and Trump, there has been a significant lack of willingness to accept these results because they did challenge what many had come to rely upon in the world and with power. And for the political scientists who see political marketing and advertising as the "wrapper of deceit" (Dean and Croft 2001) big data should make them happy as the statistical methods utilised by these commercial operators would not look out of place in a first-year university political science course.

Big data is not going to disappear any day soon. Regulators and legislators may one day start to put a boundary on what big data firms can do but considering that will have to be implemented by the very people that benefit from its use that may not happen for a while yet and even if it did perhaps it will just provide guidelines more than laws. This is one area that is worthy of further investigation and research from not just a big data perspective, but how these methods are changing political marketing, systems, organisations and markets, and even democracy itself.

Is Social Media Engagement a Predictor of Voting Behaviour? Breaking the Myth?

One important way in which many in political campaigning are currently in error on when it comes to social media and digital platforms is that voter engagement equals likely behaviour. It isn't and it may not be. Even though a voter sending a tweet or posting a status update may be an action, it is not proof of what that person's final behaviour may actually be. It is really only a sign of interest, as any good consumer behaviour model would testify.

In more recent times this has tripped many a campaign manager: reading the sentiment analysis from social media as a representative sample of what the population as a whole was thinking. Considering how busy people are right now, and the appeal of social media, this is only an accurate reflection of people who (a) may be on social media, (b) may actually be clearly identified and not anonymised in some way and (c) willing to go in front of potentially millions of strangers on earth and share their point of view on a topic.

Whilst sentiment and content analysis of social media is a very useful resource for measuring and understanding voter behaviour in political marketing and advertising, it is only one measure, it is not *the* measure. If anything, what may be lacking is a broader model of consumer behaviour in political marketing that reflects how consumers have changed their behaviour in politics with the advent of technology and different ways in which they access and retrieve information. The conceptual models that will be discussed in Chap. 8 will go someway to addressing this issue.

Another issue to consider on social media as a predictor of behaviour is that consumers are responding to an advertisement or communication by another actor on a political issue or topic. This is not an indicator of final behaviour or brand loyalty, unless it is expressed as such, but more of an attitude or emotional response towards the advertisement. Valenzuela (2013), who examined protest movements, found that the higher the level of engagement, the more likely that was to lead to a person taking the next step in the behavioural process but it could not be used as a predictor of what that outcome would be.

Therefore, any response towards a political advertisement should be scrutinised more closely to see if that is a response towards the issue, advertisement or mentioned brands or even all three. Suffice to say though that hitting like on a social media page means very little compared to the more robust metrics such as view time, sharing or comments and, as Valenzuela (2013) found, this is only a sign of where a person is in the behavioural process, not how they may vote in an election.

PRACTITIONER IMPLICATIONS

For practitioners the lessons from this chapter are that social media is becoming an important tool in relationship building, organising supporters and volunteers, donations and motivation. It can also be used to move a consumer along in a behavioural process through exposure to communications, user-generated content and greater engagement and sense of experience with other users and the brand.

As for television advertising, however, caution should be used with negative advertising as this may have a more amplified effect on social media due to the higher engagement many users have on these platforms and how it may act as a motivator for further negative behaviours and a demotivator for others who otherwise may have been engaged with the brand.

The potential of social media is still limitless and as further applications come out to meet more specialised needs this may help with greater targeting and personalisation of messages at the cost of the further splintering of markets.

CONCLUSION

Social media is the future of political advertising and political marketing as a method to create relationships, organise a campaign or brand, a robust marketing research tool and as a motivator for all users. Yet it is no silver bullet or miracle cure for the current ills of political advertising.

It is still at the mercy of those who run campaigns and their philosophy on how they see the use of political advertising—a weapon of mass consumption or a bridge between brand and consumer that will allow co-creation of value, a sharing of experiences and engagement, and a creator of emotional responses that can then be attached to the relationship to further strengthen it.

REFERENCES

Cadwalladr, C. (2016, December 4). Google, democracy and the truth about internet search. *The Guardian*. Retrieved from https://www.theguardian.com/technology/2016/dec/04/google-democracy-truth-internet-search-facebook

Cannon, D. A. (2002). The ethics of database marketing: Personalization and database marketing—If done correctly—Can serve both the organization and the customer. (Business Matters) *Information Management Journal, 36*(3), 42–45.

Dean, D., & Croft, R. (2001). Friends and relations: Long-term approaches to political campaigning. *European Journal of Marketing, 35*(11/12), 1197–1217.

Heath, R. (2017, September 21). EU Confidential Episode 14: NationBuilder's Toni Cowan-Brown—German election—Boris Johnson's fact and fantasy. *Politico*. Retrieved from http://www.politico.eu/podcast/eu-confidential-episode-14-nationbuilders-toni-cowan-brown-german-election-boris-johnsons-fact-and-fantasy/

Jones, B. (2016, December 21). Meet NationBuilder, the mercenary software that powered Trump and Brexit. *Digital Trends*. Retrieved from https://www.digitaltrends.com/web/the-political-software-used-by-trump-and-the-brexit-campaign/

Lapowsky, I. (2016, November 15). Here's how Facebook actually won Trump The Presidency. Retrieved from https://www.theguardian.com/technology/2016/dec/04/google-democracy-truth-internet-search-facebook

Lapowsky, I. (2017, June 20). What should (and shouldn't) worry you in that voter data breach. *Wired*. Retrieved from https://www.wired.com/story/voter-data-breach-impact/

Milne, G. R. (2000). Privacy and ethical issues in database/interactive marketing and public policy: A research framework and overview of the special issue. *Journal of Public Policy & Marketing, 19*(1), 1–6.

Schlegelmilch, B. B., & Öberseder, M. (2010). Half a century of marketing ethics: Shifting perspectives and emerging trends. *Journal of Business Ethics, 93*(1), 1–19.

Schmitt, P., Skiera, B., & Van den Bulte, C. (2013, May). *Referral programs and customer value*. American Marketing Association.

Solomon, M., Hughes, A., Chitty, B., Marshall, G., & Stuart, E. (2013). *Marketing: Real people, real choices*. Pearson Higher Education AU.

Thaler, R. H., & Sunstein, C. R. (2008). *Nudge: Improving decisions about health, wealth, and happiness*. Yale University Press.

Valenzuela, S. (2013). Unpacking the use of social media for protest behavior: The roles of information, opinion expression, and activism. *American Behavioral Scientist, 57*(7), 920–942.

CHAPTER 6

Mobile Political Marketing and Mobile Political Advertising

Abstract Mobile political marketing and advertising has been around for two decades now, but it is still one of the most dominant methods in this area. SMS, for example, is an important part of every US Presidential campaign, and is a vital tool in engaging and involving voters and volunteers in developing nations. This chapter discusses the rise of mobile marketing in politics and the transformation from SMS to multimedia messaging and apps on mobile devices that parallels the growth in smartphones and tablets in many parts of the world.

Keywords Mobile marketing • SMS • Android • Apple • Political marketing

INTRODUCTION

Mobile marketing has revolutionised marketing from the time the first mobile phone became accessible to mass markets. Whilst back then most phones were restricted to just short message services (SMS) or multimedia messaging services (MMS), the development of smart devices such as the iPhone, iPad and iPod was the pivotal change in this area.

© The Author(s) 2018
A. Hughes, *Market Driven Political Advertising*,
Palgrave Studies in Political Marketing and Management,
https://doi.org/10.1007/978-3-319-77730-6_6

All of a sudden consumers could carry a truly portable computer in their pockets or handbags that had the power of a laptop, the functionality of a camera, and the ability to share and upload content, experiences and emotions through multiple social media applications. Not to mention the literally thousands of other applications that can be used on a smart device.

There is a divergence of thought when it comes to mobile marketing. Some see smart devices as being just platforms through which consumers access an application on the move, a temporary experience between perhaps more fixed experiences on desktop devices or traditional media such as television and print. In this line of thinking mobile devices are simply one way out of many that a consumer accesses information and content.

Others see mobile marketing as being truly revolutionary for consumers and brands alike, being able to target consumers directly in a full immersive real-time experience that allows for engagement in ways that were not possible even 10 years ago when the Obama campaign of 2008 was the first to use YouTube as a key part of a campaign strategy. Consumers can use mobile devices to search, engage and create information with other consumers across the globe in seconds, which has had a significant change on how brands now undertake marketing and reinforced a changing view on the dominant paradigms in marketing and communications.

Perhaps one way to see these two lines of thought on mobile marketing is to see them as being reflective of generational attitudes and perceptions towards mobile data and media itself. Not everyone is on Facebook but most under the age of 40 probably are, if Facebook's own stats are any guide (Statista 2018).

This chapter will take a broader approach to discussing mobile marketing, starting off with the older methods of SMS and MMS that are still in use in many parts of the world today.

It will then move to a discussion on devices, apps and platforms and just how these three aspects of mobile marketing have combined to change how we as consumers now spend our time and gather information.

It will conclude with a brief discussion on how and why mobile marketing has been and is changing political marketing strategy and campaigns across the world, using examples of campaigns where mobile marketing was an important dynamic in the success or loss of candidates or a party.

Short Messaging Service (SMS) and Multimedia Messaging Service (MMS)

Short messaging service is still, as on the date of writing this book, the most profitable and widely used data service on mobile devices. First created in 1985 as part of a Global System for Mobile (GSM) communications, with the actual first message sent in December of 1992, its use has spread to now where it is worth globally an estimated US$100 billion annually, although SMS has been integrated into many mobile messaging applications such as WeChat, WhatsApp, Viber, Snapchat and countless social media applications.

The legacy of SMS is seen in other applications to this day, with some seeing the SMS character limit as being the forerunner of Twitter as the initial 160 character limit. The 160 character limit for SMS is still used in many parts of the world, and has helped keep messages short and to the point, in itself a characteristic that became part of the modern era of campaigning built around easy-to-remember slogans. SMS changed political communication strategy from the time it was introduced and used by a mass market, being the first technology to allow for non-verbal real-time communications and sharing of information amongst a peer network.

Although some may argue (probably only those that could afford to use them) that pagers were also able to do this, their cost made them inaccessible to many, especially to those belonging to lower socio-economic statuses and in developing parts of the world. And pagers, apart from their widespread use in sitcoms and movies of the era, had limited application, other than for being used as a one-directional way of contacting someone.

The uptake of SMS though was helped by being made accessible through the first affordable mobile devices, primarily phones, and the ease of use in adopting the technology, requiring only a small level of patience for a user to find the right letter on the alphanumeric keypad of the phone. The first emoticons were used in SMS as keypads also contained symbols that enabled a user to create messages containing symbols and not just letters and numbers.

Cost of messages was far cheaper than other forms of communication, and, even in some nations where actual call costs to mobiles were high, it became the most used form of instant communication.

SMS and Political Campaigns

In political campaigns SMS had an immediate impact, although there is no agreed date or campaign on when the first SMS was used and where—perhaps those that have an idea can contact the author. It does appear that by 2008 that SMS in political campaigns was widespread throughout the world, including Finland (Leppäniemi et al. 2010), Malaysia (Sani 2009), the Philippines (Wu 2015) and of course the Obama campaign of 2008 where every available technology was used to reach and engage with as many targeted audiences as possible.

SMS designed campaigns realise the advantages and power of being able to cheaply, quickly and readily use a messaging service that targets voters directly and personally, whilst at the same time overcoming any technological barriers such as internet speeds. Compared to other types of communications and platforms, especially in the hyper-digital age that we now live in, SMS is still seen as one of the best methods to engage with people.

In Bernie Saunders campaign of 2015 people who attended campaign rallies and events were asked to send text messages to his campaign as this was far easier and quicker to build a database from and relied less on volunteers writing down details or being distracted from discussing policy with a voter (Corasaniti 2015). Obama of course famously announced his choice of Vice President, Joe Biden, through a text message that was estimated to have read by over 3,000,000 people in the hour it was sent (Corasaniti 2015).

The power of text messages is also evident through their ability to act as a form of fundraiser, with campaigns able to ask for donations to be sent via SMS (charged back to a phone bill usually), though this has only been possible in the United States since 2012 when the law was changed.

As an example of fundraising through SMS Obama in 2012 asked people to give $10 through texting a code number back to his campaign, with the phone user then needing to reply yes when a confirmation message was sent back to ensure the donation was made (Tantango 2016).

In the United States and many other nations caps have now been placed on donations via SMS to limit any potential negative behaviour or unknowing (it was the kids!) use of phones. If anything the use of SMS has been important in the shift in political fundraising from large donations to the micro-donations (amounts between $0–$30 or local equivalent) that are now the hallmark of many a campaign.

In the modern era, with so many other messaging apps being used, SMS is still an excellent and effective method at getting a voter's attention but also in getting their immediate engagement. With some people following sometimes thousands of people on each of the multitude of social media apps that they may use, SMS cuts through the clutter of notifications and is usually read with a higher priority by a user and therefore can be used as a direct call to arms.

The Trump campaign, for example, used SMS as an effective method of getting supporters to engage on social media when he was giving an appearance at an event or debate, as did the Cruz campaign (Tantago 2016). This is turning supporters from passive to active, and making them not just part of the campaign but also part of the value co-creation process. Supporters of the Hillary Clinton campaign demonstrated this when some set up a specific website (textsfromhillary.com) that focused on the messages that she sent and that they then helped share through memes or other posts on social media that were designed to help the campaign and garner more interest.

SMS of course has long been used in a political management perspective through organising volunteers, supporters and candidates. It was critical to the use of the first really integrated databases that combined voter information with location and issue tracking, and to this day can allow any campaign to compete with larger parties through personalised messaging that averages around 1c per message sent (Tantago 2016).

The advent of the smartphone and device mobile marketing has advanced far beyond the capabilities of the mere SMS and has lowered mobile campaigning costs to even a fraction of that of an SMS. The remainder of this chapter will now briefly discuss mobile marketing and apps.

Devices, Apps and Platforms

A Brief Background or How You've Lost Your Time and Mind Since 2007

SMS was soon followed up by MMS and the use of cameras on phones started to take off in the early 2000s when the first low-cost models began to hit the market. Whilst functionality was initially limited to static images, soon video could be recorded although the quality was restricted to 2 megapixel (MP) image files, which were very grainy and not near-broadcast quality or able to be integrated into a campaign, not to mention the cost of sending and receiving these messages were high and dependent upon decent network coverage.

The market-killer moment was of course the release of Apple's iPhone in 2007 which not only had a 2MP camera, but also had with it apps and storage that could be used to easily make video and image content, even though network coverage and costs meant that not many could afford to send or receive files away from their home wifi networks. The portability and ease of use meant that adoption quickly spread throughout the world, and soon cheaper market competitors, such as Samsung's Galaxy range that used the competing Android platform, began to hit the market and make this technology available to all.

Where early phones may have allowed only a handful of SMS to be saved, these phones allowed for gigabytes of storage, and depending upon the operating system used, came with access to thousands of applications on a virtual storefront. It was access to these applications that really changed mobile marketing and mobile devices as now consumers had the ability to do all of the same tasks they did on their computer in a mobile environment.

It was the release of devices with this capability that acted like a rocket for the growth of the social networking, messaging and sharing websites and applications that are now integrated into nearly every facet and moment of our lives. The introduction of tablets, such as Apple's iPad and Samsung's Galaxy Tab range, developed markets even further and brought a bigger screen experience to consumers that more closely matched what they enjoyed through a laptop or desktop PC.

All of a sudden user experience (UEX) and user interface (UI) became the new tech buzzwords as brands sought to differentiate themselves not just on what they were actually providing, but the uniqueness of that experience and interface. In fact it could be very well argued that the UEX and UI has become the sustainable competitive advantage for so many brands around the world such as Facebook, Google and Twitter.

By the mid-2010s consumers in many developed nations had a three-screen experience at home, television, a tablet and a phone, all competing for their attention, along with of course family or other sources of attention such as a radio or stereo. All of a sudden people's lives became "busy" in an electronic sense, with every hour of a day filled with electronic information and custom-designed feeds.

Apps, Memes and #hashtags: Mobile Marketing and Political Campaigns

Political information didn't need to be accessed anymore through a news bulletin from a limited number of sources but could now be tailormade to the consumer's own preferences and included everything from the less formal Buzzfeed or Huffington Post to the more in-depth and formal sources such as Politico, Vice News, CNN or a myriad of traditional news outlets that had found new life online.

Critically though, in a mobile political marketing context, news has now become accessible wherever a consumer had a device and internet access. As technology advanced and costs lowered consumers also had near-broadcast quality capability in their camera phones and could even livestream events for an extremely low cost or even free, a political marketers dream, or nightmare, as now they could actually make the news and control messaging.

But so could everyone else, which made keeping track of what competitors were up to harder than it ever had been. This was reflected in message management as well with several low-cost news organisations now producing content from a myriad of perspectives. Social media further amplified this effect as now news production was no longer restricted to just those in the media but instead could now be anyone with a keyboard and access to the internet.

This trend has not gone unnoticed in politics: 60% of supporters of the leader of Britain's Labour Party, Jeremy Corbyn, used social media as their main source of news and Bernie Sanders received 42% of Facebook mentions compared to 13% for Hillary Clinton (Phillips 2016). These trends are duplicating that of how consumers source news in general: through mobile devices either at home or outside. According to Techcrunch (2017) US consumers now spend 5 hours per day on mobile devices, with application use now making up 92% of this time (Perez 2017). Of this, users now spend nearly an hour on Facebook every single day of the week. Another report from global research company Statista showed that in every nation smartphone use had grown to the point where now globally the number of mobile users now exceed desktop users.

What this means from a practical political campaign perspective is that when it comes designing websites and applications consideration needs to be given to how someone will access that information on a mobile device as this will directly effect how effective those methods are going to be. User experiences and interface will have the same impact on the effectiveness of a campaign as will a television advertisement, if not more by the time you've finished reading this chapter.

And secondary to that, but still vitally important from a political information and communications perspective, is how that information will be shared and read on a social media site on a mobile device, especially Facebook.

There is no mistake that applications such as Twitter, Snapchat, WeChat, Instagram, YouTube, Pinterest and a realm of other applications should also be considered for use by those in political marketing, and in fact if recent campaigns from around the globe are any guide they are already in good use and application.

With the development of these apps though it isn't just news that is shared. Images and videos are becoming more and more critical if the uptake of apps of this type, such as Instagram and YouTube, are any guide. Facebook has been used to launch new policies on live video streaming, such as in 2017 when legislation regarding marriage equality by the Australian Prime Minister was announced, turning mobile devices into sophisticated direct marketing tools at any time of the night or day.

SMS may have started the ability to build databases and engage with supporters, but more advanced integrating messaging apps, such as Facebook and Google+, allow for the integration of other data, such as behavioural, location, time and demographic information, that can build a more complete picture of the political consumer and how they respond to political advertising and marketing in campaigns. The use of hashtags on sites such as Twitter and Instagram is an example of how a consumer not only engages with political information on mobile devices but also how that can then allow a political brand the chance to use that data to build a more complete picture of a consumer using data provided by mobile devices.

Campaign apps, now common in many markets around the world but pioneered by Obama in 2008, add another method of collecting data and integration with voters. Similar to Obama's SMS announcement of his running mate in 2008, in 2012 it was the Republicans' turn for innovation when Mitt Romney's campaign used the Grand Old Party's election app to announce who his Vice Presidential running mate would be. According to the Romney campaign at the time, people were more likely to engage with their campaign through the app than their Facebook and Twitter accounts (Petronzio 2012).

Many apps are now sophisticated and offer a multitude of information, media, shareable content such as memes and wallpapers, the ability to make donations and of course the opportunity to volunteer or support a campaign and then track how that support has made a difference to the campaign in the local area, which is what the Obama 2012 app did (Petronzio 2012).

This is helping make mobile marketing an ideal tool in a political campaign for micro-targeting and clustering as not only can consumers be targeted through what their interests are, but also through other pieces of information that only mobile marketing can provide. A political campaign manager could in effect make a campaign more localised and have a more authentic and natural grassroots feel for a fraction of the cost of even a small campaign run just using traditional methods from only 15–20 years ago.

However, there are many parts of the world where the use of an app or smartphones is still in its infancy due to developmental, technological, economic and societal reasons. As these parts of the world catch up and adopt technology and capability of that enjoyed by first-world nations, the use of apps as a means of political information and communication will also catch up with that now seen elsewhere. These factors, combined with the success of apps in terms of fundraising, organising and harnessing support for campaigns now being documented across the world, will see mobile political marketing and advertising only increase in use and importance to political campaigners all around the globe.

References

Corasaniti, N. (2015, August 18). Texting comes of age as a political messenger. Retrieved December 27, 2017, from https://www.nytimes.com/2015/08/19/us/politics/presidential-campaigns-see-texting-as-a-clear-path-to-voters.html

Leppäniemi, M., Karjaluoto, H., Lehto, H., & Goman, A. (2010). Targeting young voters in a political campaign: Empirical insights into an interactive digital marketing campaign in the 2007 Finnish general election. *Journal of Nonprofit & Public Sector Marketing, 22*(1), 14–37.

Perez, S. (2017, March 3). U.S. consumers now spend 5 hours per day on mobile devices. Retrieved January 7, 2018, from https://techcrunch.com/2017/03/03/u-s-consumers-now-spend-5-hours-per-day-on-mobile-devices/

Petronzio, M. (2012). Politics transformed: The rise of mobile in election 2012. Retrieved December 30, 2017, from http://mashable.com/2012/10/02/mobile-election-2012/#F2uq1A6j7uqs

Phillips, A. (2016, February 9). Social media is changing the face of politics—And it's not good news. Retrieved January 3, 2018, from http://theconversation.com/social-media-is-changing-the-face-of-politics-and-its-not-good-news-54266

Sani, M. A. M. (2009). *The public sphere and media politics in Malaysia*. Cambridge Scholars Publishing.

Statista. (2018). Distribution of Facebook users worldwide as of April 2018, by age and gender. Retrieved April 30, 2018, from https://www.statista.com/statistics/376128/facebook-global-user-age-distribution/

Tantago.com. (2016, February 2). 2016 candidates capitalize on SMS donations. Retrieved January 5, 2018, from https://www.tatango.com/blog/2016-candidates-capitalize-on-sms-donations/

Techcrunch. (2017). US consumers now spend 5 hours per day on mobile devices. Retrieved December 12, 2017, from https://techcrunch.com/2017/03/03/u-s-consumers-now-spend-5-hours-per-day-on-mobile-devices/

Wu, I. S. (2015). *Forging trust communities: How technology changes politics*. JHU Press.

CHAPTER 7

Political Advertising: Practitioner Lessons for 2018 and Beyond

Abstract Political advertising is an evidence-based field. Many practitioners provide research and data which guide research and thought in the area and this chapter aims to do exactly that: how prior evidence discussed in the book can provide a guide for a practitioner that may want to run a campaign in the modern era.

Whilst not strictly a DIY guide for campaigners, it reminds practitioners that politics and campaigning should focus on a market driven, people first philosophy, and not just the ability to show that you are cool because you have an app.

Keywords Political campaign • Political advertising • Grassroots campaign • Political service quality • Political experience

HOW TO RUN A POLITICAL ADVERTISING CAMPAIGN IN THE DIGITAL ERA

To run a successful campaign in the current markets around the world it is just no longer enough for a party to undertake a market-focused, market-driven approach—they need to have an integrated marketing strategy for all of their activities from policy formulation and candidate selection through to communications and management of the organisation itself.

A. Hughes, *Market Driven Political Advertising*,
Palgrave Studies in Political Marketing and Management,
https://doi.org/10.1007/978-3-319-77730-6_7

There are parties, including many minor ones, who may think that their platform and values mean more than marketing to the mainstream or winning over the masses. However, this is a matter of perspective, as regardless of size, system or platform running a successful campaign in an election is more about understanding that there should only be a small gap in how they are defined by their market and how they in turn define their market. The AfD in Germany is a party that does keep this gap to a minimum, as do the Greens in many places around the world. Being a good political marketer should not be something that is unique, but something that is common.

Keeping this market perspective and focus in mind makes life far easier when it comes to running a political advertising campaign in the market-driven era of politics. As discussed, earlier political advertising is no longer just a tool for awareness building and reinforcement of relationships. By using modern technology it is becoming a tool for creating experiences, establishing and maintaining brand resonance and personality that develops brand loyalty and engagement beyond the short window of a campaign.

Critically though it is also becoming a form of live market research and information gathering, a truly two-way communication method. If anything modern political marketing methods favour minor parties who can use them as a way of being perceived as being more natural, authentic and engaged, and therefore as having more market focused policies. Even if major parties do something similar, their expectations of service quality mean that they struggle to achieve these same perceptions.

The information age is the dawn of a new age for political advertising, and the data in it the new currency that can be used to create information and knowledge that can transform a brand from minor player to government maker or influencer.

Therefore, these points need to be kept in mind in this chapter for this is perhaps the most practitioner focused of the entire book. Whilst not strictly a DIY guide to running a political campaign, it does seek to provide some evidence-based support for using one method or strategy over another. However, it is hoped that the balance between practitioner and theory is kept firmly in the practitioner's favour in this chapter. A simple checklist (not model but in order) that a political brand should follow if they want to implement a more market-focused approach is as follows:

1. Political advertising effectiveness can only be maximised as part of broader integrated marketing or branding strategy or being market focused

2. Research early and research often to understand the market, the issues that matter to them and how to engage with them
3. Grassroots and digital grassroots can be still powerful change agents
4. The Importance of Information: Learn from the old and use the ways of the new

   (a) Old: Information Receivers New: Information creators and seekers
   (b) Old: Television and radio advertising New: Videos and podcasts
   (c) Old: Media Management New: Media and internet influencers

5. Some models to implement

   (a) Political Service Quality
   (b) Political Experience Model (unique, exciting, engaging, vision)
   (c) Political Customer Engagement model

6. Political Brand Personality Dimensions
7. The Permanent Campaign: Some thoughts on political management

WHEN DID HAVING A MARKET FOCUS AND BEING MARKET DRIVEN = POPULIST POLITICS?

Suddenly being a market-driven and market-focused party is seen by some as being a negative, populist politics or poll-driven politics, a short-term outlook that fits the fictional Frank Underwood model of politics of some.

However, perhaps, it was the perception of democracy that needed to be examined more harshly. According to the Economist's Intelligence Unit's definition of full democracy there are only 19 nations on earth that meet that definition. Excluded from the list are the United States and France, with Norway being acknowledged as the world's most complete democracy. Yet around the world there have been countless surveys that reveal trust in government is at near-time lows, especially in nations that are full democracies such as Australia and Iceland.

And when did government of the people, by the people, for the people, as Abraham Lincoln once said, perish from the democratic minds of so many? If anything, this form of democracy is more consistent with the use of political marketing methods such as advertising and communications than concentrating power in the hands of the elites regardless of their outlook or platform. Whilst democracy as we once knew it may be dead, political marketing has given new life and perspective to political systems around the world (Hughes 2014), being an enabler of change and opportunity for many parties where once there was none. Being elected is one thing but being a permanent and relevant voice that can be heard above the noise and that can enable and influence change is perhaps sometimes more effective.

Being a market-driven party is about meeting the expectations and needs of those who support the party. With political service quality (Dann and Hughes 2008) becoming an important influence on voter behaviour in the modern era, this is not a bad thing. It is a good thing as it demonstrates that the party is engaged, actively listening and taking a relationship approach to those who support it. It reinforces the strength of the relationship and keeps the party relevant to those who are behind it. Many members of larger parties feel that they are losing relevance to their hierarchy or to the interests of more powerful and better organised stakeholders such as lobbyists, business or union groups, or other interests in society.

Keeping a market focus also keeps all relationships in perspective, as outlined in the Hughes Stakeholder Model of Political Marketing in Chap. 2, and ensures that the party does what it can to maintain each. For larger parties being populist is critical to demonstrate to the wider market that if elected to rule then they will not lose touch or connection with those who put them there and that they take a longer term view on relationships.

Therefore, before using any of the methods that will be discussed in this chapter, it is important to begin with the market focus because being popular with supporters and voters has never been a bad thing in politics, especially when using marketing methods and techniques such as political advertising.

Start Early and Engage Always

There are two approaches for implementing the market-driven party or campaign approach. The first is for new brands, the second for established brands.

For new brands the process can begin even before the launch. This can be through market research, direct engagement with an interest group with similar ideology or views, or even as a result of a breakaway from an established brand that is perhaps starting to lose its resonance with the market. The Greens parties around the world, for example, came from the broader environmental movement and the far or alt-right campaigns of recent times also have their foundations in movements that wanted a more unified and politicised platform from which to advance their perspective.

For established brands this process could begin with changing the philosophy to be market and external facing, rather than focused on internal stakeholders or the power elites. One step in making this happen would be by adopting a political service quality and relationship perspective, or by trying to obtain a greater understanding of marketing and branding methods and techniques. France's National Front did just this when it changed leadership from father to daughter and made it to the Presidential run-offs in 2017 against Emmanuel Macron from the new market-focused brand of En Marche!, which had also used market-focused policies and perspectives. The French elections of 2017 were noticeable because of the rise of the more market-driven parties, although other results in 2017, such as in Germany, New Zealand and in the Czech Republic all note the rise of the market-driven brand in politics by new and established brands.

Regardless of the approach or age of the brand, stakeholder engagement is key to obtaining the support of the early followers or the innovator-adopters of the political market. In the perspective of the market-focused brand stakeholder engagement should be treated as a form of customer engagement. Different methods of customer engagement should be used as appropriate to the market the brand targets, including more grassroots methods.

Grassroots

Grassroots methods are the tried and tested campaign and communication methods that have proven to be successful around the globe regardless of the system. For example, in Japan where there is little televised political advertising, communication is done through meet and greets on streets, in shopping centres or other public spaces. Leaflets and even old-style trucks with billboards and speakers are also widely used, along with the presence of digital methods that have wider appeal to younger markets.

Canberra (Australia) and Berlin (Germany) share something in common by allowing the near-unregulated use of roadside signs and corflutes, a method which for some communities, acts not just as an indicator of brand loyalty but of tribal loyalty.

Public speaking and events are another important way for a brand to connect with the base or the core market. US President Barack Obama was a noted public speaker, and none were better at symbolism than his speech at Selma, Mississippi, on 7 March 2015 that marked the 50th anniversary of the civil rights march to Montgomery across that bridge. It was

Obama who turned speeches from a lectern into experiential moments, intimate moments in the round that offered unparalleled engagement with the leader of the free world.

Tony Blair in the United Kingdom was a noted public speaker, and around the world there has been recognition (Gregor and Macková 2015) of the importance of speeches in meeting communication objectives. In the digital age a speech can also be recorded live, and captured for later updating to social media sites for sharing and tracking responses.

Digital Grassroots Applications

Digital grassroots political communication can be defined as being:

Any method of digital communication that allows a non-paid user to create, design and share content on a platform that can be readily seen by others and that ultimately influences behaviour.

There are many users who contribute to campaigns without even having to leave their homes or offices. Recent revelations from campaigns in the United States, the United Kingdom and other locations across the world also reveal that these grassroots contributors may not even be from the country of the campaign that they are trying to influence. Sometimes they can be from people in similarly aligned parties or movements, sometimes just perhaps concerned groups or individuals.

However, regardless of the motivation behind a contribution for many a campaign these people provide a critical source of resources on digital platforms. One of the biggest disadvantages for a party using digital methods is that they need to provide content. Content generation is not as easy as just uploading a television ad or speech to YouTube or Facebook but should allow those who support the brand to upload and share content to create engagement and demonstrate that the brand listens to the concerns of its stakeholders.

Whilst many of these methods have been discussed earlier, it needs to be understood that there is no silver bullet or one best fits all method. A political brand should consider using as many methods as are appropriate to the markets that it is targeting, and then allow the market to create content for it. Whilst not all content will be appropriate, most should and can help extend the reach of a brand into markets where perhaps it may not have had a foothold.

User-generated content also has higher credibility than brand material as the attitude towards the content is different and the message more believable than one that comes from a political brand or one that perhaps is not yet known by the target market. Higher credibility of these types of messages make them more likely to be shared and a good tool for micro-targeting and segmenting.

Although creating trust is now too hard of a task in politics, when it comes to keeping a political brand in an engaged and interactive relationship with stakeholders social media is well worth the investment.

THE LESSONS OF OLD, THE WAYS OF THE NEW

As has been noted earlier, political advertising is moving from what is still the dominant delivery platform, television, in response to the market doing exactly the same thing.

The other big change a campaign manager needs to keep in mind is how these platforms, not just political advertising, have altered how people around the world consume information. Information is on demand 24/7, in a format that can be understood in many languages, downloaded, captured, stored, shared, commented on and liked. There also has never ever been as much freely accessible information as there is at this very second in time and that is only increasing, despite firewalls, paywalls and a wide range of nasties of using the internet.

The implications of the information age for political communications is that any communication needs to be simple as possible, as short as possible and focus on a positive value offering that can be tangibly connected by the consumer to a change in an experience or their life. Even a recent study of members of Congress found that only 6% could remember the last piece of legislation that they examined (Congressional Management Foundation 2017).

This era is about building and engaging. Without a doubt most negative information and advertising is easily bypassed and overlooked, and unless specifically motivationally relevant is next to useless. This is enforced by the findings from research that has used psychophysiological measures that indicates that instead of acting as motivators towards a desired behaviour, negative communications only entrench and develop higher feelings of negative attitudes towards all forms of political communications.

Those who use negative advertising blindly because everyone else does are merely following the Hot Hand Fallacy (Gilovich et al. 1985) and failing to understand how communications and advertising work in the modern era—a frustration noted by Lord Saatchi when he took over the Conservative Party's advertising and communications strategy.

So in a concise way here are some lessons of old and ways of the new that a campaign manager should consider before launching head first into a campaign communications strategy.

Old: Information Receivers New: Information Creators and Seekers

In the days not so long ago the political consumer was an information receiver. Political advertising was a reminder of the brand, a reinforcement of its core values and platform, and the main contact anyone had with a political brand. For the supporter or undecided it was seen as an information resource along with the media, friends or other credible sources. Sadly as time and time again parties failed to meet the core service expectations promised before an election, the credibility of organisations and political leaders and candidates disappeared into the abyss and what once worked no longer had the same effectiveness across all the previous metrics, although as an awareness tool it is still unchallenged with the older demographic.

Outside politics times and credibility changed how information was treated by a consumer, regardless of that being about a car or cancer. Now consumers only have a limited capacity for processing any message and anything that is not motivationally relevant is going to be lucky to last more than just a few hours in the short-term memory of a consumer. Hence part of the reason why negative advertising no longer is as effective as it once was: it just isn't relevant or interesting enough for most people to watch (Hughes 2016).

As has been noted in studies in political communication, the trend towards the power of an image over other forms of information has increased markedly since the digital age began. A cunning campaign director could choose to exploit this situation by using misinformation, or the new era description of fake news, as a method against opponents by capitalising on a consumer's lack of information and knowledge of a topic to influence and alter behaviour by aligning the fake information with the negative perceptions of a brand. For example, saying a conservative brand will privatise a public health system because that would fit in well with what a conservative brand might do.

What this all means in a practical sense is that a campaign manager needs to avoid using negative advertising, or to use it sparingly if tempted, and keep information in a message to positive content and largely visual only in format. As a low-cost alternative user-generated content does provide a more credible and user-friendly resource for informational communications, such as videos.

Again, even with user-generated content, negative valence material needs to be kept to a minimum as the organisation needs to be creating a positive experience that reinforces the positive value offerings being made. Perhaps one strategy where negative may work is if that value offering includes removing from government or parliament a perceived damaging adversary.

Tools like infographics should be used alongside static and print advertisements as they have proven to be a good source of information for consumers and as a visual form of communication would have greater significance and impact over the more traditional mediums. Radio advertising can be used in a far more targeted way, and should be combined with the use of podcasts and other digital audio as a way of providing information and content to consumers, especially through mobile platforms. This will assist in enabling a more casual, conversational way of engagement and maintaining positive stakeholder relationships.

Old: Media Management New: Media and Internet Influencer

A once infamous Australian politician described media management as feeding the chooks. Typically Australian it could be said, but the days of chook feeding are well and truly over.

Media management now includes not just the various traditional or heritage platforms such as television, radio and print, that are still very influential, but also social media applications and websites. A former White House Press Secretary during Barack Obama's term in office described his job as being more like message control than media control in the era of social media.

Whilst a modern political brand will provide full content, even interviews, to media outlets that themselves have undergone dramatic industry change and disruption with the change in the availability and quantity of information and will usually edit to fit content rules, message control is still an important tool for any political communications campaign.

Integrated with the content generation discussed earlier, political organisations have also become news outlets, posting their own stories, news, information and events on their various social media channels. A campaign director with a low budget, even one in the hundreds of dollars and not thousands, could easily do exactly this and should.

Messages can now be influenced by using internet influencers, or those who are famous on social media sites and have followings that sometimes reach into the millions. Campaigns don't usually explicitly incorporate these people into communications as instead they have far more impact through sharing their support on a social media site. Using hashtags helps link the supporter to the campaign in a more credible way. A campaign manager should ask for the more famous supporters to undertake this strategy, even a simple "selfie" with a candidate or leader can be enough to build support and engagement for a campaign.

IDEAS FOR THE CAMPAIGN MANAGER

This section discusses ideas a campaign manager may consider in relation to improving the consumer's perceived service quality, expectations and delivery on the perceived brand performance. In the service age that now exists it is vital for politicians to start to begin to understand how they are meeting the expectations of voters and supporters on the services that they provide.

Linked into this concept is customer engagement strategy. Political brands need to rethink engagement and adopt more commercial strategies to develop stronger relationships and resonance with their consumers. This may reduce the use of political advertising as this has become the utility tool for too much in political marketing and instead put the focus back on other methods to achieve electoral aims.

Next, the experience that a political brand provides also needs to be considered as part of a campaign or wider communications strategy. If this can be integrated with service quality and engagement a political brand can start to develop more effective communications by integrating a clearer brand personality and positioning across different media and advertising strategies.

Finally what personality consumers perceive and identify the brand as having is another tool to consider for a campaign manager, and one that will influence the advertising strategy.

Political Service Quality

Political Service Quality (Dann and Hughes 2008) is something all political managers should consider implementing and measuring on a continuous basis. As Vargo and Lusch (2004) noted over a decade ago, and before them Grönroos (1997) and Prahalad and Ramaswamy (2000, 2004), the world is becoming a service-centric place.

Politics is no different. In fact, one of the reasons why faith and trust in government and political parties is falling is because they don't see that they are failing to provide the services that they promised in order to get elected. It can be contended that opinion polls, which can include preference, satisfaction and approval levels, are also measuring levels of service quality and performance.

Politics may be in the era of the permanent campaign (Blumenthal 1982, Needham 2005) but it is not isolated by consumers from how they interact with other service providers. Perhaps if this was integrated and used more in politics then there would be less issues around perceived service provision. Brands could also focus much more on service delivery outcomes in advertising and reinforce more clearly connections between behaviour and value exchanges.

Communications between elections could also be used to highlight either opponent's service failings or focus on how a brand would provide better service if elected.

Political Customer Engagement

Political Customer Engagement is an adaptation of a more commercially focused customer engagement model (Brodie et al. 2011, Van Doorm et al. 2010) to politics. With permanent campaigning a party should be constantly engaged with their target market, although the level of that engagement may alter according to where a brand is in the election cycle.

Yet the modern political consumer is more active on issues than ever, even if that activism is from the relative safety of an anonymous user name on the internet. This modern activism demonstrates that the political consumer is active and willing to engage and be engaged with all the way through the political cycle and not just during elections. Chapter 8 discusses some models that may be useful when it comes to ways of analysing how to improve engagement but also where a consumer may be in the process that eventually leads to relationship and desired behaviour.

For the practitioner, though, the Van Doorm et al. (2010) model provides a good way to assess how it can start to improve political customer engagement. Table 7.1 provides a summary of this model and should enable a practitioner to start to consider ways in which they can better engage with the market. In a way this is ironic that a political actor who

Table 7.1 Simplified customer engagement model (adapted from Van Doorm et al. 2010)

Antecedents →	Customer engagement behaviour →	Consequences
Customer based • Satisfaction • Trust/commitment • Identity • Consumption goals • Resources • Perceived costs/benefits	• Valence • Form/modality • Scope • Nature of impact • Customer goals	*Customer* • Cognitive • Attitudinal • Emotional • Physical/Time • Identity
Firm based • Brand characteristics • Firm reputation • Firm size/diversification • Firm information usage and processes • Industry		*Firm* • Financial • Reputational • Regulatory • Competitive • Employee product
Context based • Competitive factors • P.E.S.T.		*Others* • Consumer welfare • Economic surplus • Social surplus • Regulation • Cross-brand • Cross-customer

should be concerned with obtaining the votes or desired behaviour of actors would need to know customer engagement foundations but yet as O'Cass (2001) notes, not many political organisations have marketing knowledge within them, even though they are interested in doing so.

Political Experience Model (Unique, Exciting, Engaging, Vision)

If a campaign manager is reading this then one of the most important things to do in a marketing promotions sense is to make your brand an experience. Consumers want experiences and not just opportunities to consume or buy something. Experiential marketing (Schmitt 1999) is becoming more and more important for all brands, but especially for those seeking to develop deeper emotional relationships and resonance with consumers. According to Schmitt (1999) there are five strategic experiential modules that can be used in creating an experience in marketing, outlined in Table 7.2.

Although Schmitt's (1999) modules can be used in politics, there are some special characteristics of politics that may make some slight additions necessary. For example, considering the importance of loyal consumers in politics, especially for minor parties and independents, providing an experience that is unique, exciting, engaging and provides an aspirational vision that acts as a strong motivator of behaviour is important to the long-term viability of these organisations and for a vibrant democracy in a Western system.

Even in a non-Western system, consumers still want to experience something that is unique, exciting, engaging and has aspirational appeal. Nearly all consumers can remember one such experience such as this in their political consumption lives. Maybe it was Jacindamania in New Zealand, Kevin07 in Australia, Obama's Hope campaign, Blair and New Labour in the United Kingdom, France's En Marche!, Trudeau's Real Change or Change Together, and the list goes on across the world. What they all had in common was those ingredients.

But the campaign managers also acted as though they were in charge of a tech start-up and used far more entrepreneurial and commercial methods to make their campaigns unique, engaging and viral, creating a sense that supporting them was an opportunity to be part of something unique or even historical that may not happen again. That they may not have received more votes probably highlights how loyalty and commitment works in politics more than a critique of their campaigns.

Table 7.2 Schmitt's strategic experiential modules (adapted from Schmitt 1999)

Strategic experiential module	Description
Sense	Consists of the five senses, sight, sound, touch, taste and smell.
Feel	Relates to a consumer's feelings and emotions from an experience.
Think	Relates to the ability of an experience in delivering either a problem-solving or engaging cognitive experience.
Act	Relates to experiences that target our behaviours, lifestyles and attitudes (think about segmentation here).
Relate	Is about the desire for a consumer to be part of a social context or something that they can relate to others with.

Table 7.3   Political strategic experiential modules (adapted from Schmitt 1999)

Strategic experiential module	Description
Feel	Relates to a consumer's feelings and emotions from an experience.
Think	Relates to the ability of an experience in delivering either a problem-solving or engaging cognitive experience.
Act	Relates to experiences that target our behaviours, lifestyles and attitudes (think about segmentation here).
Relate	Is about the desire for a consumer to be part of a social context or something that they can relate to others with.
Sense of change	Relates to how the vision and engagement with the brand creates a feeling of being a part of positive change.
Leader	Relates to how experiences with the leader support key leadership traits and notions of change and vision.

The lesson from these campaigns for other campaigns is don't be afraid to experiment and change the brand to better match market expectations, and create something unique that the target markets want to be part of. This is why positive messaging is more powerful as a communications tool than negative messaging.

Therefore, a simplified list of modules of experiential marketing that could be applied in politics is given in Table 7.3.

Political Brand Personality Dimensions

It is one thing to create a political brand from nothing, but it is entirely another to create a brand personality that closely matches that of what the party or person stands for.

Brand personality researchers (Aaker 1997) have noted the importance of developing characteristics that will give the brand a distinct personality that can act as a source of competitive advantage in a crowded market. However, as political brands are either people or built around them this makes creating a brand personality more unique to politics as the party brand need to be consistent with the leader brand.

This has been one of the consequences of the "leaderisation" or Presidential-style politics (Poguntke and Webb 2007)—party brands have largely moved away from ideological platforms to more issue-based ones to ensure that they can be more consistent with the personal beliefs and styles of their leaders.

Table 7.4 Brand personality types (adapted from Aaker 1997)

Sincerity	Excitement	Competence	Sophistication	Ruggedness
Down to earth	Daring	Reliable	Upper class	Outdoorsy
Wholesome	Spirited	Intelligent	Charming	Tough
Cheerful	Imaginative	Successful		
Honest	Up-to-date			

Brand personality dimensions should be built around the key political leader dimensions of competence, leadership, integrity and empathy identified by Garzia (2011). These could be merged with one of Aaker's five types of brand personality to develop a leader brand that can help develop closer resonance and relationships with consumers through developing a brand personality that a consumer can identify as matching their personality when it comes to that product. Table 7.4 provides a table of brand personality types that may be used by political brands and can be used to match up with certain brand profiles being sought by consumers. Consumers will try where possible to match-up their own perceived or desired personality in a product category with the brand's (Table 7.4).

Having a strong brand personality can be a good source of a sustainable competitive advantage and aid an organisation if it wants to pursue a brand extension or perhaps a branded house strategy as this simplifies the process and lowers the cost, for example, running candidates in local or regional campaigns around similar themes.

Party brand personality dimensions could be built around key party brand dimensions on ideological spectrum—caring, more left, looking after the economy, national security, immigration, right, greens environment, and then correlated with Aaker's (1997) personality scale to again get the right match with the leader but perhaps to also maximise market reach and attraction.

If a brand can get this right then this will help consistency between messaging and brand, make life easier when it comes to developing a unique experience for the consumer and help with planning and resource allocation for campaign and political management.

Permission Marketing

One of the more interesting areas of research is the development of permission marketing. First pioneered by Seth Godin (1999), permission marketing, which is the marketing done for, with or to a target market with their explicit permission, has been widely adopted by many in commercial marketing.

In political advertising this has translated into a rival of sorts of some grassroots methods that many in the digital age have overlooked or excluded because they lack that tech innovative feel or simply because they are targeting markets where these methods may not be effective on, such as Gen Y.

Some of these methods are phone calls, SMS, hard copy mail or snail mail, and even information or town hall-style meetings. In areas where technology is still years behind the developed world or even where the market has not rapidly adopted digital applications or social media, these methods are still widely used and very effective as the market has given their permission to being contacted and marketed to.

Integrated with a pull campaign and less of a push campaign as was the hallmark 20 years ago, and recognising that these are ways the consumer wants information, these methods can be effective and definitely should be considered by any size campaign.

The key to remember here though is that it must be done with permission of the user. If not this is no longer permission marketing but annoying marketing.

Market Research and Database Management

As discussed in Chap. 5, one way a campaign can conduct marketing research in a variety of ways for a very low cost are as follows:

- Hashtag, trends and sentiment analysis of social media applications
- Metrics (views, time spent on page, likes, comments, shares, etc.) obtained from the brand's own social media accounts
- Marketing intelligence gathered from engagement with customers and supporters such as online forums, meetings, events and other direct contact
- Secondary sources such as news sites, research papers, media, opponent's positioning strategy, overseas trends and other appropriate resources.

Whilst these are low cost, they can take significant time to sift the raw data into information that can be useful for the campaign, so having some friendly volunteers to help with these tasks is a good idea.

The next level up in market research and analysis starts to turn a small campaign into a more sophisticated campaign capable of rivalling the larger parties through the integration and creation of databases. This is through using a software programme such as NationBuilder.

Whilst the lower cost account provides a significant amount of functionality, the next level of account, which only costs a couple of thousand dollars, can provide a lot higher level of integration of different social media platforms and analysis. It would be wise for a campaign to consider reducing their marketing and advertising spend by this amount to achieve this level of functionality, even at the expense of other activities.

Over time this information would produce a longitudinal study of data, information and trends for the brand that would help it identify ways in which it could engage with existing markets and attract new ones. For a small resourced party or candidate, even at the level of a micro-party run out of a lounge room, this is possible. There are free databases that also can be used, but NationBuilder has been designed specifically for those involved with political and movement-based organisations and therefore would help transition even the smallest party from amateur to more organised offering.

CONCLUSION

This chapter has provided practitioners with an overview of some marketing theory and evidence that they can apply to their brands and organisations as a way of creating a political market orientation through using political marketing methods. This chapter is not intended as a DIY guide to a campaign but rather to highlight some of the techniques that can help a party become more market focused in the digital age and lessen the reliance upon just communications and advertising as a way of achieving electoral outcomes.

It is hoped that if practitioners implement some of these ideas then society will stand to benefit from having far more market oriented brands which have a higher level of service and value creation for all stakeholders. This will lead to the evidence that researchers need to start to establish future research directions but also how these strategies and methods could be further improved and adapted to the unique characteristics of political marketing, management and branding.

References

Aaker, J. L. (1997). Dimensions of brand personality. *Journal of Marketing Research, 34*, 347–356.

Blumenthal, S. (1982). *The permanent campaign.* Simon & Schuster.

Brodie, R. J., Hollebeek, L. D., Jurić, B., & Ilić, A. (2011). Customer engagement: Conceptual domain, fundamental propositions, and implications for research. *Journal of Service Research, 14*(3), 252–271.

Congressional Management Foundation. (2017). State of the Congress. Retrieved from http://www.congressfoundation.org/projects/resilient-democracy-coalition/state-of-the-congress

Dann, S., & Hughes, A. (2008). Australian political marketing after Kevin07: Lessons from the 2007 federal election. *Monash Business Review, 4*(1), 34–37.

Garzia, D. (2011). The personalization of politics in Western democracies: Causes and consequences on leader–follower relationships. *The Leadership Quarterly, 22*(4), 697–709.

Gilovich, T., Vallone, R., & Tversky, A. (1985). The hot hand in basketball: On the misperception of random sequences. *Cognitive Psychology, 17*(3), 295–314.

Godin, S. (1999). *Permission marketing: Turning strangers into friends and friends into customers.* Simon and Schuster.

Gregor, M., & Macková, A. (2015). Euroscepticism the Czech way: An analysis of Václav Klaus' speeches. *European Journal of Communication, 30*(4), 404–417.

Grönroos, C. (1997). Keynote paper From marketing mix to relationship marketing-towards a paradigm shift in marketing. *Management Decision, 35*(4), 322–339.

Hughes, A. (2014). *The relationship between advertisement content and pacing on emotional responses and memory for televised political advertisements.* Doctoral thesis, Australian National University.

Hughes, A. (2016). Why negative political ads don't work on Gen Y. In P. Moreau & S. Puntoni (Eds.), *NA—Advances in consumer research* (Vol. 44, pp. 309–314). Duluth, MN: Association for Consumer Research.

Needham, C. (2005). Brand leaders: Clinton, Blair and the limitations of the permanent campaign. *Political Studies, 53*(2), 343–361.

O'Cass, A. (2001). Political marketing-An investigation of the political marketing concept and political market orientation in Australian politics. *European Journal of Marketing, 35*(9/10), 1003–1025.

Poguntke, T., & Webb, P. (Eds.). (2007). *The presidentialization of politics: A comparative study of modern democracies.* Oxford University Press on Demand.

Prahalad, C. K., & Ramaswamy, V. (2000). Co-opting customer competence. *Harvard Business Review, 78*(1), 79–90.

Prahalad, C. K., & Ramaswamy, V. (2004). Co-creation experiences: The next practice in value creation. *Journal of Interactive Marketing, 18*(3), 5–14.
Schmitt, B. (1999). Experiential marketing. *Journal of Marketing Management, 15*(1–3), 53–67.
Van Doorn, J., Lemon, K. N., Mittal, V., Nass, S., Pick, D., Pirner, P., & Verhoef, P. C. (2010). Customer engagement behavior: Theoretical foundations and research directions. *Journal of Service Research, 13*(3), 253–266.
Vargo, S. L., & Lusch, R. F. (2004). Evolving to a new dominant logic for marketing. *Journal of Marketing, 68*(1), 1–17.

The Future: Directions for Researchers and Practitioners

Abstract Chapter 8 finishes the book by providing a brief wrap of the ideas, concepts and evidence discussed in earlier chapters. Using these and other works as its basis it provides some work-in-progress conceptual models for political advertising and marketing for researchers and practitioners to discuss and, as long as everyone is nice, debate.

It concludes with some thoughts on the need to maintain an open network of those who research and practice in the field so that evidence can provide the bedrock in which thought and ideas in research can be built.

Keywords Political marketing conceptual models • Political branding • Brand emotional response model • Policy and issue adoption curve

Conceptual Models

Political marketing is a growing area of interest to many in research, practice and society. It is a unique area of marketing and one that provides an opportunity to test the theoretical and ethical limits of some of the more widely adopted marketing theories. For example, whilst service marketers

© The Author(s) 2018   121
A. Hughes, *Market Driven Political Advertising*,
Palgrave Studies in Political Marketing and Management,
https://doi.org/10.1007/978-3-319-77730-6_8

discuss, and rightly so, the importance of co-creation of value with other actors (Vargo and Lusch 2008; Lusch and Vargo 2014), in some political systems this may not be ideal for society and may even be used to justify the concentration of power in the hands of elites or entrench existing hierarchical structures.

This is not to limit the application of this theory in politics because if followed it can lead to strong outcomes for many. But at the same time with a market that has much apathy and little involvement or interest with politics unless it is about an issue that concerns them directly is it wise to ask them to create value when that may mean policies that only benefit some and not all, or even lack the depth to be used and implemented successfully as a government programme or policy.

One of the greatest concerns in a practical sense of political marketing is that there are very few ethical boundaries seen in practice regardless of where it is practised. Many have noted the increasing fears of policy development being sacrificed for short-term pursuit of electoral objectives and keeping the market happy with the brand at the expense of sometimes taking a harder, more rational approach to policy development that can be required in many areas of government. Politics has become more about the short game whereas good government is usually about the long game.

With those concerns in mind, and also recognising the potential of political marketing to keep democracy vibrant in mature markets such as the full democracies noted by the Economist Intelligence Unit, the models that will be proposed are done so to allow the growth of political marketing. They also recognise that in some parts of the world where there may not exist full democracies, political marketing has instead become that democratic outlet, offering a form of political expression and engagement that allows those societies to have more peaceful and rational policy discussions that rival that of any in a more Western-style democracy. In fact, perhaps some may argue in those societies that political marketing more effectively allows for a representation of a diversity of opinion that allows those nations to develop without causing long-term divisiveness that can restrict their economic, social and political development.

These models have been developed and created as a way of reigniting the fire, to borrow an expression from Harris et al. (2007). They are not replacements of existing theories or specific critiques of them, but more a realist grounded theory approach to explaining some of the more unique phenomena that characterise political marketing, branding and management in the modern era.

BRAND EMOTIONAL RESPONSE MODEL—POLITICS (BERMP)

The brand emotional response model for politics (BERMP) is a conceptual model aimed at recognising how consumers engage, co-create and relate with political brands (Fig. 8.1).

Whilst the model has its foundations in Keller's Customer Based Brand Equity (CBBE) model (Keller 2001), in no way is this intended to replace or supersede that. Instead this is a conceptual framework on how brands and political consumers respond to each other as brands try and move political consumers to a long-term relationship. It is therefore more general than specific but also attempts to encapsulate the emotional responses a political consumer may have towards a brand that is engaging with them in the hope of forming a sustainable relationship.

BERMP recognises the increasing importance of emotions in political advertising, especially the role of positive emotions and therefore advocates a more substantial use of positive advertising and promoting value gain than that of value loss. It recognises the evidence from the more successful campaigns and social movements that positive aspirational and imaginative offerings are what lead to enhanced levels of emotional responses, a greater desire to engage and a more valuable experience with political brands. These act as antecedents for attachment and relationship to the political brand.

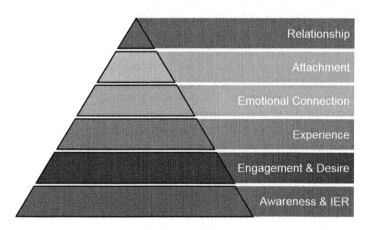

Fig. 8.1   Brand emotional response model

The first step, for example, considers how important the Initial Emotional Response (IER) between a consumer and a brand can be. This could be as simple as a meeting at the shops or on the street with a candidate or volunteer from the party. Or it could even be an exposure to politics and political advertising before they are old enough to vote but are engaged with issues and movements. However, that very first engagement and experience of a political brand is crucial in how they then respond emotionally to a brand and the communications from it.

The second step, engagement and desire, is concerned with explaining the level and intensity of desire and engagement by a consumer after their first initial experience response and awareness of a brand. This is linked to salience in Keller's model, that is, once the brand identity has been established after the first step, then a consumer should want to engage further with the brand through experiences such as media and perhaps local- or state-level voting. This further experience then creates a desire within the consumer for that to transition to the next stage of their relationship with the brand.

However, if the intensity of that engagement and experience is lacking then this makes it hard to transition to have a deeper attachment and relationship with the brand. This is why that perhaps when a new leader is chosen for a party they may not necessarily change the fortunes of a party. But it can also explain that if a leader, such as Jeremy Corbyn, can achieve a more positive level of experience and engagement then they may very well be able to turn around the fortunes of their party.

This level quickly transforms into an emotional connection with the brand that could be based around many different needs and wants that are being satisfied through the enjoyment and experience of the brand. This is not as needy as that demonstrated in desire, but should lead to an attachment to the brand, perhaps through supporting the party at a local or state level. Although this attachment may wane if service delivery fails to meet expectations, it never really disappears but morphs into a more mature attachment to the brand whose meaning and perception strengthens into unquestioned loyalty or for a political party a safe seat.

Regardless if a consumer changes their vote or swings according to their own specific needs, the party still needs to engage with the market. With this in mind parties should start designing communication strategies which engage and involve stakeholders at an earlier stage rather than when the campaign is finally announced. It should be kept in mind that this model is proposing a way to conceptualise how consumers respond to a brand in an emotional sense, and therefore guide how political advertising can be designed and implemented. An issue or specific policy is another thing entirely.

Therefore, a further conceptual model is proposed on how a consumer may adopt a policy or issue based on their engagement, experience and emotional responses with that policy or issue.

POLICY AND ISSUE ADOPTION CURVE

With the importance of specific issues to political consumers now becoming more significant in determining electoral success than a broad-based policy platform that no one can recall, and the relationship this is having on the creation, implementation and effectiveness of political advertising, this model proposes a way of conceptualising how a consumer adopts a policy or issue (Fig. 8.2).

Based on the underlying theory from Rogers's innovation-diffusion model (2010) this model incorporates the importance of some of the key concepts that have already been discussed in this book and in this chapter through BERMP. It is slightly different though as it does consider that for a policy or issue to be adopted by a consumer in the modern area there needs to be a lot of emphasis placed on engagement, experience and emotions in the early stages of adoption as these act as ways of positive reinforcement and risk reduction. The early stages also gives consideration to the importance of family, peer groups, society and individual relevance on adoption of an issue and the function that each has on engagement, experience and emotions.

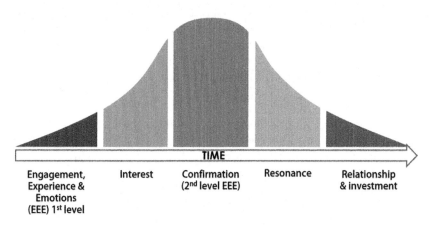

Fig. 8.2   Policy and issue adoption curve (adapted from Rogers 2010)

Interest is representative of the role consumers now have in seeking out more information on an issue. Google has become one of the world's biggest companies because we now seek out more information on a topic, not because it is given to us. Interest recognises how critical information is now in our lives, as anything that is not motivationally relevant to us is not going to be of any interest and therefore will not be allocated any resources for processing (Briggs and Martin 2009).

A consumer would then seek out confirmation of this issue having personal relevance to them through a higher level of engagement, experience and emotional response to the issue or policy. If that is achieved then they will develop resonance with the issue which then should lead to a natural evolution to relationship and investment, which may be expressed through external actions such as joining a movement, creating content via posts on social media or even voting based on the level of importance and relevance on that issue to them.

The Three Es of Political Advertising—Emotions, Engagement and Experience

Using the evidence from elections, empirical studies and the more recent research that used psychophysiological data, there are three main requirements for a successful political advertisement.

As nearly all advertising and communications models recognise, emotions play an important role in the effectiveness of a political advertisement. The problem for most political advertising now is that the pre-existing attitudes towards the advertisement and brand are so negative that using a negative advertisement to achieve an emotional response is not going to work (Hughes 2014, 2016). The recent successful campaigns in New Zealand, Canada and France, all different voting and political systems yet the same result, were noted for their use of positive advertising and communications.

Going back in political history, the most successful campaigns have come about because they were built around a positive, aspirational theme that engaged directly with the target markets and made them believe in what that campaign did. That emotional buy in to these campaigns was stronger than just a simple purchase decision for these consumers as they invested in them. That investment meant that the opponents never really stood a chance by just using the same old methods and hoping some fear appeals would get them re-elected.

So an advertising or communications appeal needs to be positive and connected to the important issues of the voter. The stronger that is, the stronger the likelihood that a voter will engage and develop a connection and resonance with that brand.

Customer engagement is also important. How is the advertisement actually engaging with the target market? Is it done in a way that they can understand and relate to? Does it contain a small amount of information so that the consumer can effectively process it and retain that in their medium- to long-term memory? These are all important questions in ensuring that an advertisement is used more as a weapon of mass consumption and less as just another 30 seconds of gibberish that no one really listens to whilst looking at their phone/tablet/laptop/significant other.

Commercial marketing realised these points a long time ago but so did politics. Obama was a good example of someone who could shake hands, kiss babies and then share all of that on social media with the right hashtags. That's effective engagement. And engagement done well creates inside the consumer a special feeling, heightening the emotional intensity in the response to the brand, but also ensuring that the consumer feels that this is now an experience they want to be part of.

Experiences are only now starting to become the focus of more research in marketing. The relationship between experiences and political advertising is in need of further research but if the findings from the profit world are anything to go by then a deep engagement and high intensity of emotional response will help create a feeling within a consumer that they are now part of a special experience. That moment is then truly co-creation of value as discussed by Vargo and Lusch (2004). It is so strong that as Schmitt (2011) notes it can be felt across different senses and ranges.

Looking back in history there have been moments in every nation's political history where people wanted to be a part of something historical, to own a piece of value, and not merely lease it as Vargo and Lusch (2004) say that an experience is. They got the merchandise, put the signs up in the yard or put a bumper sticker on their college professor's old Volvo but also put a bit of themselves into that campaign in the hope that they could say they were part of a significant change in their country.

Whilst it is hard for any advertisement to create that feeling, if it can be integrated with engagement and emotions then it can help maintain and reinforce to the consumer that they are part of something special, but also act as a reminder to those yet to support the campaign that it is not too late to do so. That fear of suffering dissonance from missing out on that sort of opportunity says that perhaps a positive message will always be more successful than a negative one.

DIRECTIONS FOR RESEARCHERS

Researchers in political advertising and marketing have several directions in which to explore this area. Whilst study in this area can be difficult due to the attitudes some have towards the increasing integration of business methods and philosophies into political strategies or the difficulty in collecting data in some nations for different reasons, political marketing and advertising is being increasingly adopted, applied and implemented in many nations around the world.

This alone is increasing the data and knowledge of how consumers in a diversity of markets are treating the use of these methods, and this has been reflected in how research centres or groups into understanding political marketing have sprung up across the world. The contributions of those who founded and pioneered these groups, such as Darren Lilleker, Jennifer Lees-Marshment, Phil Harris, Paul Baines, Bruce Newman, Aron O'Cass, the Kotler brothers, Alex Marland and Philippe Maarek to name just a few (and apologies to anyone left out—it was an innocent mistake I promise!) have all provided plenty of ideas and areas to explore. These researchers are all still making valuable contributions to the field, only in 2016 Philip Kotler, at the young age of 85, wrote a book that identified 14 shortcomings of democracy and how they need to be overcome.

In political advertising the same can be said of Michael Rothschild, Annie Lang, Frank Biocca, Travis Ridout, Fowler, Ted Brader, Gina Garramone, Pinkleton, Merritt and the late Lynda Lee Kaid to again name just a very small amount of pioneers who have set research directions and provided ideas for the generations that have or will come after them.

Yet there is still so much left to explore. Some of the points raised in this book already note the need for further research and exploration, either as theory as a whole or in more specific national or regional contexts that can add knowledge and interest to the field.

Further research into how consumers actually watch political advertising is one area that needs more attention. Many prior studies in political advertising have studied responses in controlled environments—primarily at a university—and asked participants to watch one advertisement at a time and then fill out a survey. This is hardly replicating what happens in the real world and therefore provides practitioners with a false sense of security when it comes to the effectiveness of some communication strategies. This is not how consumers watch anything and nor is it replicating what really happens when a consumer thinks about or views political advertising.

The use of psychophysiological methods, where the laboratories resemble someone's lounge room and insert ads into an ad break in a show as how a consumer would watch television or the internet and capture responses in real time, is adding more rigour and validity to political advertising research in the modern era. For political advertising researchers out there reading this, using as close to real-world environmental conditions through these methods is recommended as it may reveal some very interesting findings about how political advertising stimulates (or doesn't) emotional responses.

On social media platforms an advertisement is likely to have maybe 5–15 seconds of exposure before it is skipped and the primary content watched. And this can happen in an environment perhaps as mobile as the device being used to watch the content itself: train, bus, tram, walking, coffee shop or somewhere else. Whilst it is hard to replicate these environments they do need to be noted as how a political consumer may watch an advertisement, but research does need to start to examine how watching political advertising on mobile devices impacts on responses, experience and engagement with political advertising. This is especially so for the shorter advertisements of a handful of seconds as mainstream advertising research itself still needs to do more research into the effectiveness of these types of ads on these types of platforms.

Researchers should also consider the time effect of political advertising on social media—is there an optimum time to have an ad on social media and, if so, does this time alter for the issue being promoted? Research by Facebook has found that people tend to write optimistic posts on Friday to Sunday, so perhaps if a party was promoting a more positive message would they better place their ads on a weekend when voters may have a better reaction to it? And are they more or less likely to click on an ad on a weekend or during the week? These may seem like practitioner-focused topics but they would also aid researchers into understanding how this soon-to-be dominant platform actually can be used effectively.

Whilst the list could go on nearly forever, the final area of need of research in the next decade would be the role of information in political advertising. Whilst many have approached this in a more rational or information-receiving context, there has been far too little research done into the type, amount, format and structure of information used in political advertising. This is despite increasing work being done on these topics in the neighbouring disciplines of communications, advertising, cognition and neuropsychology. This will require the use of more advanced research techniques, such as psychophysiological experiments, to gain an insight into how information is consumed by the political consumer and other actors. As a guide, researchers should consider some of the topics that Annie Lang has provided in her articles on this area that could quite easily be applied and investigated in political advertising.

Researchers also have another role in this area. To discuss with their colleagues and practitioners what areas are in need of priority for investigating and exploration, and perhaps even publish a top-ten style list of hot topics for research. Sadly some academics are becoming overly protective of ideas and research, when what this area needs is those who are prepared to innovate, share and discuss ideas, evidence and opportunities with each other without fear of abuse or dodgy behaviour. Perhaps the best thing that political advertising researchers could do here is do a better job at promoting their field.

Directions for Practitioners

For practitioners the previous chapters have provided insights into what direction political advertising is headed in. To recap, social media, whilst growing at exponential rates in use, quantity and understanding, is a long way from being the dominant form of political advertising—for now. This will change over time as generations age and technology takes more and more control of all aspects of our lives.

However, practitioners need to learn how social media and political advertising can work well with each other, be that platforms, methods or strategies. Content creation and generation needs to be further explored. For example, building databases and using apps such as NationBuilder will be critical in the future to understand how political advertising works on digital platforms. It will also lay the foundation for increasing the effectiveness of political communications by providing the information of what is required to achieve better emotional responses towards political advertising.

The use of different forms of political advertising to different segments also needs to be explored. Are apps and certain types of social media more appealing to younger generations? And does direct marketing still have higher effectiveness rates on older markets than social media? Is a podcast or a vidcast the more appropriate media for different types of target markets? And how much time does it take to maintain and run a full service political website compared to one that may offer less information and interactivity? These are all questions practitioners need to start asking, and answering, as digital takes hold but also as more heritage methods still demonstrate a high degree of effectiveness and reach.

Practitioners also need to be more careful with negative advertising. If some social media public opinion polls run by media organisations are anything to go by then over 80% of people have a strong dislike for it. That number grows to the 90% range if the dislikes are then included (Hughes 2016). Practitioners should start to experiment much more with positive advertising and what methods and strategies can be used to integrate it successfully with the broader campaign.

Traditional forms of political advertising, such as outdoor and hard copy materials, also need to be retained but adapted and integrated much more effectively into digital advertising and the wider campaign itself. One of the more notable issues of political advertising from a practitioner perspective is how methods seemed to be used and analysed in isolation. They are definitely part of the much bigger campaign and it is worth remembering that the political consumer still sees the same shopfront or brand image regardless of that appearing in hard, soft or any other type of copy such as skywriting.

In conclusion, regardless of the method don't be afraid to be innovative, to be bold and to go where no other campaign has been before, if that is what makes your campaign work. Plan before execution and keep the central theme and story of the brand in mind before designing or implementing any advertising. And finally remember that advertising is only the communication of the value offering. The value offering itself is what will win the campaign, the advertising just makes people aware that you exist and that they have in you someone they can engage and share an experience with and like enough for them to commit their vote and time to.

CONCLUSION AND FINAL WORDS

Political advertising is far from dead. It is alive and fluid as the politics now happening in many parts of the world reveal. Whilst there is much excitement over how digital and social media has changed political advertising, it is still about communicating the value offering to the market and it still needs to do that as effectively as possible for the party or candidate to gain enough support to meet their electoral objectives.

With the changes in markets, consumers and technology there is a need to start to create new models and new ways for how political advertising can be effective but also more innovative in these modern times. This chapter has provided some conceptual models, mainly hoping that they provide ideas for practitioners, discussion and likely debate for academics, and better advertising for those who consume political communication in their homes/workplaces/public transport/some other location.

As political advertising is a part of the bigger marketing world, some of the models in this chapter also examined concepts and theories in which political advertising can nest, such as branding, customer engagement and service quality. Researchers often have the benefit of time when it comes to investigating political advertising, but practitioners don't so it is hoped that they follow the directions discussed above sooner rather than later.

With political advertising only growing in use and application around the world, and regardless of political system or nation, there will certainly be no shortage of material to analyse in years to come, or those willing to investigate it and inspire and assist all those in this field with their findings.

Final Note

Thank you. To whoever you are right now reading this. For making it this far. This project could not be what it was without you, and people like you, showing an interest in the area of political marketing and advertising. May you prosper and go far in this field. And finally, it's been emotional. So don't blame me for voting for Kang and not Kodos.

References

Briggs, K. E., & Martin, F. H. (2009). Affective picture processing and motivational relevance: Arousal and valence effects on ERPs in an oddball task. *International Journal of Psychophysiology, 72*(3), 299–306.

Dann, S., Harris, P., Mort, G. S., Fry, M. L., & Binney, W. (2007). Reigniting the fire: A contemporary research agenda for social, political and nonprofit marketing. *Journal of Public Affairs, 7*(3), 291–304.

Hughes, A. (2014). *The relationship between advertisement content and pacing on emotional responses and memory for televised political advertisements.* Doctoral thesis, Australian National University.

Hughes, A. (2016). Why negative political ads don't work on gen Y. In P. Moreau & S. Puntoni (Eds.), *NA—Advances in consumer research* (Vol. 44, pp. 309–314). Duluth, MN: Association for Consumer Research.

Keller, K. L. (2001). Building customer-based brand equity. *Marketing Management, 10*(2), 14–19.

Lusch, R. F., & Vargo, S. L. (2014). *The service-dominant logic of marketing: Dialog, debate, and directions.* Routledge.

Rogers, E. M. (2010). *Diffusion of innovations.* Simon and Schuster.

Schmitt, B. (2011). Experience marketing: Concepts, frameworks and consumer insights. *Foundations and Trends® in Marketing, 5*(2), 55–112.

Vargo, S. L., & Lusch, R. F. (2004). Evolving to a new dominant logic for marketing. *Journal of Marketing, 68*(1), 1–17.

Vargo, S. L., & Lusch, R. F. (2008). Service-dominant logic: Continuing the evolution. *Journal of the Academy of Marketing Science, 36*(1), 1–10.

INDEX

© The Author(s) 2018
A. Hughes, *Market Driven Political Advertising*,
Palgrave Studies in Political Marketing and Management,
https://doi.org/10.1007/978-3-319-77730-6

Printed by Printforce, the Netherlands